Praise for
TURNAROUND: AVOID BANKRUPTCY
AND REVITALIZE YOUR COMPANY

BY EDMOND P. FREIERMUTH

". . . a book from which all entrepreneurs can benefit. It reads quickly and provides insights into situations many entrepreneurs and business owners find themselves in without having had the opportunity of preparation. No one likes to contemplate a company's failure but the sad fact is that many companies do fail, and frequently because the chief executive officer did not know (in time) many of the facts and elements depicted in this book."

—ARTHUR LIPPER III,
Chairman and Publisher
Venture Magazine

"This book is a superior one for any business person, but it is especially valuable for any entrepreneur interested in survival planning . . . authoritative . . . should be read by all executives; even those who head purportedly healthy companies."

—*Insurance Advocate*

"This book should help managers spot serious financial problems before a company goes over the brink."

—*The Cleveland Plain Dealer*

"This is a great strategy book for a manager or owner of any business, but it is *must* reading for those involved in turning around a troubled company. Take it from a CEO who's been pushed to the brink—and survived."

—BYRON A. ROMIG, Jr.,
President and CEO
Bymac, Inc.

"This is a book you can use to find and check your business pulse."

—*Video Store Magazine*

"His book shows managers and business owners how to recognize the signs of impending financial difficulties and how to take steps toward renewing financial stability and business strength."

—The Journal of Commercial Bank Lending

"This very practical and easy-to-read book describes a results oriented approach to turning around a company in financial trouble. I speak from experience when I say that the author knows what he is talking about. Ormand Industries probably remains in business today because we followed his tough-minded, but accurate, advice on cash flow management."

—JARRELL D. ORMAND
Chief Executive Officer
Ormand Industries, Inc.

"Our company got into deep financial trouble. We followed the five turnaround steps outlined in this book, dealt with our angry stakeholders, reorganized (without bankruptcy court proceedings), and re-established our good name in our community. Turnaround management and Ed Freiermuth are synonymous."

—H. EDWIN LYON
Chairman and CEO
Allied/Lyon Companies, Inc.

Turnaround:

Avoid Bankruptcy and Revitalize Your Company

Turnaround:

Avoid Bankruptcy and
Revitalize Your Company

Edmond P. Freiermuth

LIBERTY HOUSE®

First Edition • First Printing

Library of Congress Cataloging-in-Publication Data

Freiermuth, Edmond P. (Edmond Peter)
Turnaround : avoid bankruptcy and revitalize your company / by Edmond P. Freiermuth.

p. cm.
Includes index.
ISBN 0-8306-3043-0
1. Bankruptcy. 2. Corporations—Finance. 3. Corporate turnarounds. I. Title.
HG3761.F74 1989
658.1'—dc19
88-36499
CIP

TAB BOOKS Inc. offers software for sale. For information and a catalog, please contact TAB Software Department, Blue Ridge Summit, PA 17294-0850.

Questions regarding the content of this book should be addressed to:

Reader Inquiry Branch
TAB BOOKS Inc.
Blue Ridge Summit, PA 17294-0214

David Conti: Acquisitions Editor
Katherine Brown: Production

This work is dedicated to all of the book and magazine
editors who have kindly extended to me the privilege
of writing for their distinguished publications.

Contents

Preface

Turnaround: Avoid Bankruptcy and Revitalize Your Company began life as a hardcover book. I'm delighted to say that the book achieved its fair share of critical acclaim. The book is based on methods developed in the successful consulting practice that I established in 1982 to assist businesses tangled in a web of seemingly inescapable financial problems. My methodology has proven itself successful in case after case.

This book is intended to assist owners and managers in their efforts to achieve a rapid and successful business turnaround, or, preferably, to avoid in the first place the necessity for one. More specifically, the book will show readers how to:

- Recover from serious financial difficulties;
- Save tens, if not hundreds, of thousands of dollars in legal, consulting, accounting and other fees and costs associated with business turnarounds;
- Use proven, time-tested methods of problem recognition and resolution;
- Retain a pro-active, rather than reactive, stance throughout the turnaround process;
- Utilize a few simple financial tools to implement and monitor the progress of the turnaround;

- Avoid the pitfalls of bankruptcy; and
- Emerge from financial difficulties a stronger business capable of renewed growth and sustainable profitability.

In short, it will facilitate your efforts to prepare for the worst, while planning for the best.

The message in this book is as true today, if not more so, than it was when it was originally published. As the October, 1987, stock market crash provides sobering evidence, the world economy in general and the U.S. economy in particular remains in a fragile condition. The circumstances now are very similar to those that existed at the beginning of this decade, and the consequences could very well be the same. In short, we may soon experience a recession. In my opinion, there is little, if anything, that fiscal and monetary authorities can do to ward off the economic downturn.

There is, however, much that business owners and managers can do to insulate themselves from the effects of a slumping economy. That is one of the primary issues addressed in this book. Liquidity and positive cash flow are the keys to survival, and *Turnaround: Avoid Bankruptcy and Revitalize Your Company* will show you how to achieve the results you and your creditors want.

Turnaround: Avoid Bankruptcy and Revitalize Your Company can be viewed in two ways. First, it is a look back at what happens to a company that gets into such serious financial trouble that it can't escape its problems without radical changes. Like the overwhelming majority of my clients, you will probably find that the book is effective in presenting programs for attacking already existing, hard-core business problems.

There is a second, and I think preferable, way to evaluate the utility of the book. It can also be used as a system to deal preemptively with small problems that, left unattended, could develop into serious ones threatening the survival of the business. The recurring theme that I hear from my clients goes something like this: "If only I had acted faster to implement the changes that were necessary!" Ego stands in the way of jettisoning unprofitable business activities that cannot justify their continued existence. Indecision may be the key to flexibility, but it can also lead to business paralysis and then failure. Think, then act, is my continuing admonition to owners of troubled firms.

Where do financial problems begin? They start with cash-draining, losing operations, of course. When a business incurs operating losses that diminish its capacity to honor financial obligations, it finds that relationships vital to its continued existence become increasingly strained. The loss of key vendors, customers, employees or the confidence of the company's primary source of working capital (usually its bank) can severely weaken the health of the business.

Perhaps that should be intuitively obvious to the owners and managers of businesses having financial difficulties. Maybe. But during my nearly 20 years of experience in financing and advising small and medium-sized businesses, I have found that dealing with problems that don't have well-defined solutions is one of the most formidable challenges confronting managers.

The learning method of this book incorporates doing along with understanding. Readers charged with avoiding or managing a turnaround for their business will be encouraged to implement the systematic process described here. From the perspective of a harried owner or manager of a business in trouble, there is nothing magical or mysterious about a turnaround.

The process involves a wearisome amount of details and documentation. Those of us who work in the field of crisis management call it "grunt work." It can be dull, boring, and monotonous. A concerted turnaround effort, however, can also preserve a portion of the equity an owner has at risk in the business as well as protect other assets owned outside the business. By scrupulously following the step-by-step procedures described in this book, you will be able to approach your own business problems in a way that has been proven to be effective.

To facilitate a better understanding of the dynamics involved in a business turnaround, a ficticious, privately owned company—Zefco Container Mfg. Co., Inc. ("Zefco")—has been created to illustrate the full cycle of a turnaround. Zefco has experienced many of the financial setbacks that could befall a company, and yet it is able to achieve a successful financial reorganization outside of the bankruptcy courts.

Over the years, I have worked as a financial consultant to many different types of businesses. For example, my clients have included firms engaged in advertising, construction, high-tech manufacturing, hardware distribution, oil field services, architecture, catalog retailing, health-care maintenance, aluminum extrusion, printing, container distribution and many others. The one common denominator is that each of the businesses had experienced a severe cash flow crisis. The point here is no matter how unique or specialized you think your business is, it can be reduced to the most fungible of all commodities—cash.

Although the CEOs (Chief Executive Officers) of my clients have come from widely diverse business enterprises with significant variations in the volume of their annual sales, it has been almost uniformly true that when they read the original version of this book, they identified very strongly with the "hero" of Zefco. Many have commented that it seemed as if I were writing about *their* company, not some fictionalized account of a made-up troubled business. The truth is that when a company gets into serious financial difficulty, the problems that surface are nearly always the same. If you find yourself relating to Zefco's CEO, don't worry. The outcome of his story is a happy one, and yours will probably be the same.

Some of those who have been supportive and who have contributed to this work are R. Eric P. Allan, Bruce A. Bates, Gayle Goodman, Peter H. Griffith, Martha Hartman, Oscar J. Jimemez, Richard B. Levin, Byron A. Romig, Jr., Richard G. Shaffer, and Sarah M. Sisson.

I am also deeply indebted to the CEO's of the financially troubled businesses that have allowed me to work with them through their most trying difficulties. Their experiences were the real inspiration for this book.

Finally, and most importantly, I would like to acknowledge the contributions of my wife, Donna. Without her encouragement and editorial judgment, this work might never have been completed, and it certainly would not have been as good as people have told me it is.

Edmond P. Freiermuth
Santa Monica, California

Introduction

Texaco, Bank of America, LTV, A.H. Robins, Smith International, Wheeling-Pittsburgh, Global Marine—mere mention of the names of those corporate giants and other well publicized companies evokes a certain image of what can happen to a business when the best-laid plans do not develop as expected. Each of those corporations, and hundreds of others, are, or have been, subjects of extremely complex business turnaround efforts. With sufficient resources applied to the problems, many financially troubled businesses will survive. Regrettably though, for every successful turnaround, there will be literally hundreds of other businesses that succumb to the pressures caused by financial adversity.

The business-of-going-out-of-business has grown sharply in the decade of the 1980s. According to statistics compiled by Dun & Bradstreet Corporation, "business failures"—those businesses that stop operating while still owing money to their creditors—increased almost continuously from 7,564 in 1979 to 61,601 in 1986, by far the highest number since the Great Depression. Although the figure dropped a minuscule amount in 1987 to 61,236, it was still the second highest on record.

The most disturbing part of these data is that the U.S. economy has been expanding for more than six years—a peacetime record. Had they followed previous cycles, business failures should have long since begun to decrease. As bad as the "failure" numbers are, they may only represent the tip of the iceberg as far as the real magnitude of the problem is concerned. There are currently perhaps five to seven times as many "successfully discontinued businesses" each year as there are "business failures." There are about 300,000 to 400,000 businesses that cease to operate each year, but they are able to find a way to repay or extinguish all of their debts before closing the doors. For the business owners who have lost all, or a substantial portion, of their life's savings, it is of little comfort to know that they are not business failures in the legal, or statistical, sense. It is still a bitter pill to swallow.

The number of annual business discontinuations is likely to remain in the hundreds of thousands because so many new enterprises have been formed during this golden age of the entrepreneur. According to data published by, among others, *Inc.* magazine, there are more than 600,000 new businesses (sole proprietorships, partnerships and corporations) being formed in the United States each year. Most of the new ventures enter highly competitive markets with inadequate capital and very little in the way of formal business planning.

Quite predictably, many businesses are doomed to failure within a few years (if not months) because they quickly become unprofitable, they rapidly exhaust their working capital, and they are unable to find new or additional sources of funds (lenders or investors) to finance the business. Complicating matters further, the level of managerial training and expertise is often inadequate to deal with the myriad of internal and external problems facing all businesses, in general, and small and medium-sized businesses, in particular.

Going into business for oneself and being one's own boss has tremendous appeal for many individuals, and there are numerous publications devoted to the subject of how to start your own business. The start-up period is a thrilling time for new business owners. There is a burst of activity and excitement for everyone involved. As many sadder-but-wiser entrepreneurs have come to know, however, it is far more difficult staying in business than it is starting in business.

Chapter

1

Recognizing the Symptoms of Serious Financial Problems

Unfortunately for a great many businessess that experience financial adversity, the first real awareness that a serious problem exists occurs when a liquidity crisis arises. The most common form of this financial disequilibrium results when a business has exhausted its credit lines with vendors and its request for an additional bank loan is either met with requirements for more collateral, which is not available; or deferred, pending improved operating performance; or, worst of all, declined with the admonition that the business should seek another lender. In short, the borrower is unable to obtain further access to any external sources of working capital.

Liquidity crises rarely result from a single adverse development in a business. They generally evolve over a period of months, if not years. No matter that the process is insidious: when problems do become apparent, prompt, remedial action is required. The primary focus of this book is on the methods available for correcting serious financial problems. In this first chapter though, it would be very useful to describe how to recognize and treat the symptoms before they develop into financial cancers requiring surgery.

A successful turnaround can only be accomplished if the Chief Executive Officer of the business is willing and able to be totally immersed "in the numbers." Responsibility for financial management should not be delegated to the financial staff. The business's officers and outside financial advisors (including accountants and directors) should obviously be consulted but they should not be relied upon as surrogates for decision-making.

A key objective in having the CEO of the business learn as much as possible, on a self-taught basis, about turnarounds is that it can save literally tens, if not hundreds, of thousands of dollars in expenses normally associated with using expert outside advisors. This is not to say that consultants, lawyers, appraisers, accountants and other outsiders are not quite helpful. Rather, I suggest that much of the knowledge required to achieve a successful turnaround can be gained without having to use well-paid tutors to teach you the lexicon of a business reorganization.

The first step that many professional turnaround consultants use in identifying the symptoms of financial problems is to "spread" and analyze the historical balance sheets and statements of operations of the business. The tables which follow present the data for our mythical company, Zefco Container Mfg. Co., Inc. (Zefco).

Zefco is a privately held corporation which was started in California in 1956. During the first 20 years of its operations, the company was engaged in manufacturing various types and sizes of metal cans. (Container manufacturing is a capital-intensive business requiring expensive equipment.) In response to fierce competitive pressures during the mid-1970s, the company expanded its product line to include composite containers. In the early 1980s Zefco again responded to perceived market forces that indicated that plastic containers would dominate the container industry in the future.

Given the data shown in Tables 1–1, 1–2 and 1–3, even a novice financial sleuth (not to mention Zefco's seasoned CEO and other officers and directors) could soon deduce that Zefco has serious financial difficulties. Nearly every key financial statistic and ratio shows that the company's decline has been

TABLE 1–1

	Zefco Container Mfg. Co., Inc. Balance Sheets as of December 31, (in thousands of dollars)				
	1984	1983	1982	1981	1980
Assets					
Current assets:					
Cash	-0-	4	7	11	15
Accounts receivable	490	450	400	325	275
Notes receivable	-0-	25	-0-	-0-	-0-
Inventory	525	600	550	475	400
Prepaid expenses	65	50	35	30	25
Other	70	65	60	50	40
Total current assets	1150	1194	1052	891	755
Property and equipment, net of depreciation	2500	2250	1900	1800	1200
Other assets:					
Notes receivable (term)	-0-	25	-0-	-0-	-0-
Goodwill	368	382	396	410	424
Total Assets	4018	3851	3348	3101	2379
Liabilities and Shareholders' Equity					
Current liabilities:					
Bank overdraft	75	-0-	-0-	-0-	-0-
Notes payable (bank)	625	500	425	375	250
Current portion (term debt)	250	200	175	150	125
Accounts payable	850	750	650	550	375
Notes payable (trade)	75	-0-	-0-	-0-	-0-
Accrued expenses	25	22	19	16	13
Payroll taxes payable	50	25	20	15	10
Other	25	20	16	12	9
Total current liabilities	1975	1517	1305	1118	782
Term debt, less current portion	1750	1600	1225	1150	875
Notes payable (officers)	100	50	-0-	-0-	-0-
Total Liabilities	3825	3167	2530	2268	1657
Shareholders' Equity	193	684	818	833	722
Total Liabilities and Shareholders' Equity	4018	3851	3348	3101	2379

TABLE 1-2

Zefco Container Mfg. Co., Inc.
Statements of Operations
for the Years Ended
December 31,
(in thousands of dollars)

	1984	1983	1982	1981	1980
Sales	4821	4236	4018	4031	3807
Cost of Sales	4211	3618	3224	3055	2975
Gross profit	610	618	794	976	832
Selling, general and administrative expenses	627	508	482	443	419
Income (loss) from operations	(17)	110	312	533	413
Interest expense	454	341	326	315	210
Other expenses	20	17	15	13	12
Income (loss) before taxes	(491)	(248)	(29)	205	191
Provision (benefit) for state and federal income taxes	-0-	(114)	(14)	94	88
Net income (loss)	**(491)**	**(134)**	**(15)**	**111**	**103**

TABLE 1-3

Zefco Container Mfg. Co., Inc.
Key Financial Statistics and Ratios
for the Years Ended
December 31,

	1984	1983	1982	1981	1980
Sales percentage growth rate	13.8	5.4	0.1	5.9	—
Gross profit margin (in percent)	12.7	14.6	19.8	24.2	21.0
SG&A expenses as a percent of sales	13.0	12.0	12.0	11.0	11.0
Interest as a percent of sales	9.4	8.1	8.1	7.8	5.5
Net income (loss) as a percent of sales	(10.2)	(3.2)	(0.1)	2.8	2.7
Average accounts receivable collection period (days)	37	39	36	29	26
Inventory turnover (times)	9.2	7.1	7.3	8.5	9.5
Average accounts payable disbursement period (days)	65	65	59	50	43
Net working capital (in thousands of dollars)	(825)	(323)	(253)	(227)	(27)
Fixed asset turnover (times)	1.9	1.9	2.1	2.2	3.2
Debt to worth ratio	19.8:1	4.6:1	3.1:1	2.7:1	2.3:1

developing almost constantly for the past five years. The question that begs to be asked is, "Would any competent management team or savvy extender of credit really allow such poor performance to continue for such a protracted period?" The answer, of course, is, "Absolutely not!" What really happened to Zefco? Could the situation have been recognized earlier than it was?

Although a number of the symptoms of Zefco's financial troubles have been evident for some time, (for example a negative net working capital position and an increasing debt to worth ratio), it was not until the company's outside CPAs issued the year-end financial statement covering 1984 and 1983 that the matter was brought to a head.

Zefco's management was naturally extremely disappointed when the bottom line figures were reported by the accountants, but the company's loan officer at the bank nearly went into a state of shock because he immediately began thinking about the possible consequences of being pinned with the responsibility for managing a loan that went sour. After a restless night of thinking the matter through, the loan officer made a difficult, but thoroughly correct, decision about how to deal with the problem: confront it head-on and immediately discuss the situation with the senior credit administrator in the region.

At a regional headquarter's meeting later that day, the bank officers began assessing the seriousness of the financial problems which have befallen Zefco. They quickly discovered that the symptoms of the company's difficulties are not unlike those of virtually all businesses that get into trouble. The symptoms include the following:

- Internally prepared financial and operating data have been irregular, untimely and/or inaccurate, resulting in inconsistent reports from the company officials.
- A restatement and/or reclassification of prior period financial data as a result of changing auditors or changing the method of presentation from a "compilation" or a "review" statement to an "audited" statement.
- Unit sales volume has shown a decline in recent years.
- Selling, general and administrative expenses as a percent of sales are growing.

- Interest expense is increasing at a faster rate than sales.
- Cash flow from operations has been negative for the past few years, primarily because the business is actually losing money.
- Deficit cash flow from operations has been "financed" by trade credit and bank loans.
- An increasing amount of management's time is being used to resolve problems with vendors.
- Sales forecasting is continually optimistic while actual sales and backlog indicate a different picture.
- Accounts receivable have become progressively "stretched," resulting in increasing "ineligibles" and the irresistible temptation to "pre-bill."
- The conversion of accounts receivable to notes receivable.
- As a result of taking a physical count of the inventory, it is discovered that a "writedown" must be taken.
- The company is technically in an overdrawn position with its bank and, accordingly, is "playing the float."
- The conversion of accounts payable to notes payable.
- Payroll taxes and other funds held in a fiduciary capacity are being diverted to pressing corporate uses (like buying materials critical to filling an important order or meeting this week's payroll).
- Net working capital is negative and has continued to deteriorate.
- The company's debt-to-worth ratio has declined to the point where the company is no longer "bankable."
- Controls over purchasing and personnel are in disarray.
- Analysis of the problems is frequently focused upon external factors to the exclusion of relevant internal matters.

In short, the company is bleeding to death but the steps needed to stop the hemorrhaging are not being administered.

After listing the problem areas, the loan officer and the senior credit administrator began to analyze them in greater detail. Zefco's internally prepared financial and operating data are intended to provide management and the bank with up-to-date analyses of performance. The loan agreement between

Zefco and the bank requires that monthly financial reports, prepared by the company, be furnished to the bank; they include a balance sheet, a statement of operations, an accounts receivable aging, an inventory report, and an accounts payable aging.

A review of the bank's credit file on Zefco showed that many of the reports were not on hand. It was not immediately clear if the reports were not submitted or were improperly filed. Nevertheless, many of those that had been provided were irregular (did not conform to the agreed-upon format), untimely (the most current balance sheet was three months old), and apparently inaccurate (the statement of operations for the first ten months of the year indicated that Zefco was operating at break-even, suggesting that the $491,000 loss in 1984 occurred during the last two months of the year).

On the surface, it appears that the loan officer had not done a very thorough job in managing the credit. There seems to be a reasonable case for this initial conclusion, but a review of the loan officer's "call reports" for the past six months might indicate that Zefco's management was either unaware of, or deliberately misrepresenting, the actual financial condition of the company—a very serious matter, if true.

The reports of the meetings with Zefco officials suggested that the company was on the verge of an important breakthrough in some of its new markets and that 1985 might possibly be the best year in the company's history. How could the perceptions of Zefco's managers be so far off target? A large part of the problem rests with poor internal, and inadequate external, accounting controls and monitoring systems. The crisis at Zefco did not develop over a period of a few months: it evolved over a span of two or more years.

The seriousness of the company's problems was uncovered by Zefco's newly retained outside CPAs during the year-end audit for 1984. For the first time in three years, Zefco had decided to have a full-blown audit performed. In 1983, a compilation statement had been prepared and in 1982 the company's financial statements were reported in a review statement. (Note: compilation and review statements are not available to publicly owned companies.) Although the forms in which financial data can be presented are very, very similar, there are important distinctions among these three types of financial statements. A brief digression is needed here to explain them more fully.

In the Zefco audited financial statements for 1984, the independent CPA (among other salient factors), expressed the opinion that:

> the financial statements referred to above present fairly the financial position of Zefco Container Mfg. Co., Inc. at December 31, 1984 and 1983, and the results of its operations and changes in its financial position for the years then ended, in conformity with generally accepted accounting principles applied on a consistent basis.

Zefco's outside auditors have, in essence, lent their good names and reputations to the company, with respect to the quality and usefulness of the financial information being presented to interested parties. Users of audited financial statements have reason to believe that the data presented can be relied upon with a high level of confidence. Although the facts presented for Zefco are of an adverse nature, they are an accurate portrayal of the company's financial condition.

The financial statements compiled by an outside CPA for Zefco covering 1983 contained the following caveat:

> A compilation is limited to presenting in the form of financial statements, information that is the representation of management. We have not audited or reviewed the accompanying financial statements and, accordingly, do not express an opinion or any other form of assurance on them.

Notwithstanding this caution flag, which should have been obvious to the users of the financial statements, the form of the information presented was virtually the same as audited or reviewed statements. That is, a balance sheet, a statement of operations and retained earnings, a statement of changes in financial position and comprehensive notes to the financial statements were presented. To the inexperienced reader, it appeared that the statements were very similar to those of prior periods. The major distinquishing feature was the reliability of the data.

In the Zefco financial statement review for 1982, the following paragraph appeared in the transmittal letter sent from the outside CPAs to the company's Board of Directors:

> A review consists principally of inquiries of company personnel and analytical procedures applied to financial data. It is substantially less in scope than an examination in accordance with generally accepted auditing standards, the object of which is to express an opinion regarding the financial statements taken as a whole. Accordingly, we do not express such an opinion.

Although a review statement is of markedly greater scope and usefulness than is a compilation statement, it does have its limitations. Unlike an audit, there are no independent verifications performed with banks, customers or vendors; there is no outside observer of physical assets; and there is no test of inventory valuation. A review is good but requires that management pay close attention to the details if it is to be an effective accounting control.

The principal difference among the three types of financial statements available to privately owned businesses is the amount of time that an outside auditor needs to complete the assignment. An audit takes about two to four times as long to finish as a review, and about four to eight times as long as a compilation. Since most CPA firms charge their clients by the hour, it is obvious that compilation and review statements are considerably less expensive than are audited statements. However, as the Zefco story unfolds, we will see that the short-run savings of several thousand dollars nearly resulted in the company's failure.

Zefco's accounting controls started to slide in 1982 when the decision was made to change from an audited financial statement to a review statement. The company was about to incur the first operating loss in its history, and management was actively seeking ways to cut expenses. Although Zefco's outside CPAs advised against the change, they complied with the decision because they did not want to lose Zefco as a client, and they felt that a review could be done with sufficient care that it would not materially affect the quality and usefulness of the financial statements.

As marginal profits (or losses) continued to plague Zefco during 1983, the controls problem was exacerbated in three new ways. First, management decided to eliminate quarterly reviews with its outside CPAs. Again, cost reductions were the aim. Although this decision was strongly protested by the accountants, it was begrudgingly accepted. Second, the accounting staff was reduced by 20 percent, including the controller, who was getting burned out by the constant pressures. Despite the cuts, Zefco's accounting department was apparently able to continue grinding out the required reports.

Third, Zefco decided that it could get by with a compilation statement for 1983. (Note: Although the loan agreement with the bank stipulated that Zefco have a minimum of one review statement each year, everyone overlooked the fact.) This time, Zefco's independent CPAs for the past ten years would not go along with the change and they resigned from the engagement. This should have been perceived as a possible major problem by creditors, but it was not. Actually, it presented only a very slight inconvenience for the company because there are virtually hundreds of well qualified CPA firms that are desirous of having clients as large as Zefco. No one questioned the change in CPAs, particularly since Zefco reported a small profit for 1983. Also, the bank had enough trouble with its loan portfolio in 1983 that it was not actively looking to add new problems to the "workout" list. In brief, the loan was unwittingly permitted to decline in quality.

In late 1984, the financial and accounting controls at Zefco began to quickly unravel, and management became deeply concerned about the problem. The company was in a constant struggle to meet its payroll and pay other pressing bills. Management decided to retain yet another CPA firm, and this time they agreed to have an audit performed. The worst of management's suspicions were confirmed shortly after the audit commenced. The first order of business was to observe the inventory; the second was to verify accounts receivable.

What Zefco management thought was in inventory simply was not there. Inventory on the company's books at the end of 1984 showed $1,075,000; the outside auditors were able to account for only $725,000—a difference of $350,000. Another $300,000 in items were either severely damaged or clearly obsolete and would need to be written down. After a lengthy perusal of Zefco's books and records, it was found that the company had been (apparently innocently, but nevertheless) improperly relieving inventory when shipments of goods were being made. In other words, Zefco had been capitalizing rather than expensing overhead and other costs of production, resulting in overstated earnings. Unfortunately, because insufficient checks and balances were in place, the practice had been going on for nearly two years.

The accounts receivable of Zefco were also in less than satisfactory condition. At year end, the company books indicated that there were $560,000 in receivables. Subsequent to its verification tests, the outside auditors could only validate that there were $520,000 in payments due to Zefco, suggesting that inaccurate billing practices were being performed. Furthermore, it was determined that Zefco was carrying $30,000 in accounts receivable on its books which were of dubious collectibility and would need to be written off.

The result of maintaining poor records, systems and controls over inventory and accounts receivable meant, at a minimum, that a restatement of the financial data would be necessary and substantial losses, rather than profits, would probably be posted for 1984 and 1983. The auditors immediately brought the inventory and accounts receivable problems to the attention of Zefco's management. They were stunned! They were skeptical! They argued that there must be some mistake!

After a few days of intensive meetings with the senior partners of the CPA firm, the realities of the situation began to take hold. Not unexpectedly, the initial response of the management of Zefco was unintentional withdrawal and inaction. They wanted to wait until the full "damage" report was finished. At the completion of the audit, Zefco was faced with substantial losses and a seriously damaged financial condition.

It is now clear that Zefco's cash flow from operations has actually been negative for the past two-plus years. This fact was partially obscured because the unaudited and unadjusted statement of operations for 1983 showed a marginal profit. Had closer scrutiny of the company's balance sheet been made, however, Zefco's deteriorating financial condition might well have been detected earlier. For example, the combined growth in trade credit and short-term bank loans, from $775,000 to $1,475,000, was much greater than should have been expected given the much lower growth rate in sales volume. Additionally, net working capital was obviously in rapid decline for the past five years, even without writedowns and writeoffs. Zefco should not have allowed itself to *ever* have a negative net working capital position.

One of the tactics that managers use when cash flow is tightening is to expand its number of vendors and to lengthen its payment periods with current suppliers of materials and services. Zefco was guilty of using this approach, and for a while it succeeded. Invariably though, deficit cash flow from operations results in a business' inability to pay current liabilities as they become due. When that occurs, the pressures begin to mount. Management begins to spend more and more time on the telephone with creditors. The repeated use of the familiar refrain, "The check is in the mail," is a sure sign that black clouds are looming on the horizon.

At the same time that Zefco's accessibility to trade credit was rapidly declining, its borrowing base (80 percent of eligible accounts receivable and 30 percent of qualified inventory) at the bank started showing signs of weakness. Accounts receivable had become progressively stretched and ineligibles (accounts over 90 days) were resulting in lower availability. Despite problems with the receivables, until the inventory writedown occurred, it appeared that the bank's loan was well collateralized.

Subsequently though, it became apparent that the bank was actually in an "overloan" position. At year-end, the short-term bank note was $625,000. The borrowing base formula applied to the audited financial data showed that only $549,500 was available: [($490,000 × .8 = $392,000) + ($525,000 × .3 = $157,750) = $549,500]. Thus, Zefco's borrowings under the short term revolving credit line were $75,500 higher than permitted. To compound matters at the bank, there is a $700,000 term loan (secured by fixed assets) which, until now, has been kept current. The bank is justifiably concerned.

Zefco's financial woes are not limited to trade creditors and the bank. The company is also behind in its payments to federal and state agencies for payroll taxes. This is an especially significant problem for the owners and managers of Zefco because, although they were not aware of it, they are personally liable for the payment of these obligations. Finally, Zefco has recently become delinquent in the payment of debts related to leased vehicles and equipment, and the lessors are threatening repossession.

The owners of Zefco are very concerned for another, closer to home, reason. They have personally guaranteed all of the bank debt and some of the trade credit and other secured debt. The bank guarantees are secured by second trust deeds on their personal residences.

After completing their internal review of Zefco and confering with other bank executives, the loan officer and the senior credit administrator decided to invite the managers and owners of the company to a meeting at the bank's regional headquarters. The bank's "official" position would be that Zefco should find another lender within the next 30 days because the company's debt-to-worth ratio had declined to the point that it was no longer a "bankable" credit. (The bank knew that such a request would be extremely difficult to fulfill, but it served the purpose of placing the company on notice of what was to come if a turnaround program was not initiated immediately.)

It is obviously much easier to determine the symptoms of a business in trouble after the fact than before. Had Zefco management, the bank loan officer and/or the trade credit managers paid closer attention to what was really occurring in the business, they might have been able to change the company's direction earlier. As it is, a turnaround requiring considerable effort will be necessary if Zefco is to survive.

Chapter

2

Assessing the Causes of Zefco's
Financial Difficulties

On a Friday afternoon in late March, three days after receiving and reviewing Zefco's audited financial statements for 1984, the bank officers responsible for managing the account requested that Zefco's management meet with them on the following Monday to discuss the situation. Understandably, the company's CEO was shaken and deeply concerned. He asked his key managers to cancel their weekend plans and join him at the company's offices to help him prepare for his meeting with the bank.

Many of the symptoms of Zefco's now acute financial crisis (the extremely tight cash position, excessive growth in inventory and accounts receivable, rapidly expanding accounts payable and short term bank debt, etc.) had been evident for at least six months. Zefco's management (and its creditors) should have realized that there were problems which were not being addressed. Zefco's CEO asked his subordinates, "What happened?"

One-by-one the managers acknowledged that they sensed that something was awry, but they insisted that they were not aware of any substantive financial difficulties until the auditors dropped the "bombshell"—a loss of $491,000 in 1984 and a restatement of 1983's financial data. Zefco's managers uniformly expressed the opinion that they actually expected a small profit for the past year based upon the ten-month income statement figures they were given in early December. Indeed, the company-prepared numbers seemed to indicate that things were better than they were.

"How could that be possible in the circumstances!?" demanded the CEO.

"Maybe it's a simple case of bad accounting and controls," suggested the vice president of marketing, as the accounting manager winced.

With a glare that silenced everyone in the room, the CEO reponded, "If the answer is that easy, we'd all better get our resumes ready because the bank and our other creditors are going to think we're terribly incompetent as managers and recommend that some of us should seek other employment opportunities!" With that response, the tone was firmly set for a more serious analysis of the causes and nature of the company's financial problems.

The vice president of production offered the notion that, "The protracted recession that began in early 1980 must be one of the underlying causes of the company's troubles." He added, "You know, Zefco has always had problems during economic downturns."

Was he right? The Zefco CEO went to his office, pulled out (and dusted off) his black notebook containing selected historical data on the company's operating performance, and returned to the meeting. Like many small and medium-sized businesses, Zefco has been adversely affected by the ups and downs in the economy. The CEO shared the information shown in Table 2–1 with his junior officers.

The vice president of production was right to a limited extent. The historical financial data show that Zefco does have a history of lower earnings during recessionary periods. However, in every economic tailspin before the one beginning in 1980, the company was able to respond nimbly enough to post modest profits. Notwithstanding the fact that the most recent recession was the worst since the depression of the 1930s, Zefco would ordinarily have been expected to cope with the declining economy and then rebound sharply.

TABLE 2–1

Zefco Container Mfg. Co., Inc.
Summary of Operating Results: 1956–1982
(in thousands of dollars or percentages)

Year	Sales	Income (Loss) Before Taxes	Pretax Margin (%)
1956	$ 150	$ 8	5.3
1957	163	10	6.1
1958*	155	3	1.9
1959	180	7	3.8
1960	210	11	5.2
1961	245	13	5.3
1962*	250	10	4.0
1963	293	14	4.7
1964	331	18	5.4
1965	384	22	5.7
1966	402	20	4.9
1967*	410	7	1.7
1968	455	21	4.6
1969	507	26	5.1
1970	585	32	5.4
1971*	563	8	1.4
1972	609	19	3.1
1973	694	29	4.1
1974	802	24	3.1
1975*	775	2	0.2
1976	978	42	4.2
1977	1193	54	4.5
1978	1466	70	4.7
1979**	1884	87	4.6
1980	3807	191	5.0
1981	4031	205	5.0
1982*	4018	(29)	(0.1)

* Recession period troughs
** Purchase of former competitor completed in November 1979

At least some of the loss in 1982 could clearly be ascribed to the recession and, in view of the change from an audit to a review financial statement (for the reasons stated previously), maybe the loss recorded in that year was actually larger than initially presented. Given the robust U.S. economic growth that occurred in 1983 and 1984, though, it is unlikely that the huge losses registered in those years were entirely the result of exogenous factors. Management would need to search further from within.

"Let's be brutally honest with ourselves, shall we!" said the normally reserved and diplomatic vice president of personnel. "The primary cause of Zefco's current financial malaise was the purchase of Winco Can Mfg. Co., Inc. in 1979." (Note: Winco, like Zefco, is a fictitious company and is included for purposes of illustration.)

The CEO and the other members of management were, to say the least, taken aback by this comment. "Would you like amplify on that comment?", the CEO asked rhetorically.

The personnel manager responded, "I'd rather that someone else put his head in the noose, but, in the interest of bringing some needed focus to this meeting, I'll give you my reasons why the Winco acquisition was responsible for Zefco's troubles. First, we paid too big a premium to buy that company. Second, we used too much cash (working capital) to finance a portion of the purchase. And third, we financed most of the acquisition with debt."

"Those are pretty serious charges you're making," the marketing manager (who, incidentally, held the top marketing job at Winco prior to its purchase), blurted in an obviously defensive tone.

"All right, let's not allow this to develop into a personal matter," the CEO said.

"Fine," retorted the personnel manager, "let's evaluate the facts one at a time."

The CEO answered, "You've got the floor."

"On December 31, 1980," the vice president of personnel began, "the goodwill account on the company's balance sheet totalled $424,000. This represents, as we all know, the unamortized portion of the purchase price of Winco in excess of the net assets acquired. Based upon the annual rate of amortization in this account, ($14,000), Zefco paid a premium of $440,000 to buy the common stock of Winco. The net assets acquired were $885,000, indicating that Zefco paid the sellers a premium of nearly 50 percent over book value (the total purchase price being $1,325,000). Low tech companies simply do not command those kinds of premiums."

Fairly amazed that his personnel manager possessed these heretofore hidden financial talents, the CEO said, "Other things being equal I'd agree with you, but there are other factors to consider in the transaction. Of greatest significance, the sellers required us to pay only $200,000 in cash down, and they took back paper for $1,125,000, payable over nine years at 12 percent interest per annum. If you will recall, that was pretty cheap financing in November, 1979."

The CEO was correct in that observation. In October, 1979, the Federal Reserve Board embarked its now-firmly-established policy of concentrating on the country's money supply targets rather than interest rates as a means of achieving long term, stable economic growth. As a consequence of the dramatic shift in Fed policy, interest rates immediately began their accelerated upward spiral. The 12 percent interest that Zefco agreed to pay the sellers of Winco seemed cheap at the time. Indeed, every facet of the transaction appeared to make compellingly good sense.

Although subsequent events obviously proved otherwise, it would have been exceedingly difficult for even well trained credit analysts reviewing Zefco's business plan in late 1979 to have concluded anything other than that the company had developed a sound concept for profitable growth through expansion. During the preceding five years, both companies had posted the best results in their business histories, and the opportunities for synergistic growth seemed bright.

The personnel manager then said, "I'm not suggesting that the acquisition decision, as such, was a mistake. Rather, I'm saying that as the facts have unfolded I'm of the opinion that we paid too much for Winco. We then compounded the problem by using Zefco's limited cash resources to make the $200,000 down payment. By using some of its working capital (short-term funds) to finance a portion of much less liquid, long-term assets, Zefco created a deficit net working capital position—a situation which has worsened ever since the acquisition. Furthermore, by taking on the $1,125,000 in long-term debt we ruined Zefco's debt-to-worth ratio." (See Table 1–3.) Before 1980 Zefco virtually had no long-term liabilities.

The CEO responded with the following comment: "With inflation raging at the time, it appeared eminently sensible to finance the Winco acquisition with the 12 percent fixed rate seller loan, the interest on which is a deductible expense.

Although Zefco had carefully avoided term debt financing in its past, the temptation proved irresistible in late 1979. In addition, I think we all believed that the company's negative net working capital position would be, at worst, a short-term problem that Zefco would eliminate with retained earnings from future profits."

After pausing for a few seconds to reflect on the matter, the CEO said, "Although there a number of other rationalizations we could make for the decision to finance the Winco acquisition in the manner we did, I agree that leveraging Zefco at, what has turned out to be, the worst point in the economic cycle was a, and perhaps the, contributing factor in our current financial predicament. What else have we done wrong? Let's lay everything on the table."

The vice president of marketing, not noted for understatement, said, "I think the move into this Taj Mahal was the principal reason for our problems. I don't think it was necessary, and the timing was horrible."

The CEO did not ask the marketing manager to elaborate on the subject. He was already aware of his reasons. Back in late 1981 when the decision was made to consolidate the operations of Zefco and Winco under one roof, there had been much internal bickering; and the opposition leader was the marketing manager.

The company moved into its new plant in January, 1982. The facility was within two miles of Zefco's old operation but forty miles from where Winco was located. There was little doubt that the new facility was superior to the older plants in all physical respects: fifty percent more office and manufacturing space (the landlord also agreed to finance $250,000 in leasehold improvements at 10 percent for ten years); better lighting, power and ventilation; adjacent to a rail spur; and so forth. However, these advantages did not come cheap. The rent on the new 45,000 sq. ft. building was, and fortunately remains at, $12,800 per month. In addition—despite using many of its own employees—the cost of relocating all of the records, furniture, plant and equipment was nearly $200,000.

The combined cost of renting the two, much older facilities had been $6,600 per month. Because Zefco has been operating at less than full capacity since it moved into the new facility, the higher operating costs had an adverse effect on the company's financial results. Like many other business managers, Zefco's managers underestimated the depth and the duration of the recession beginning in early 1980. Despite substantial efforts to attract new customers and retain old ones, 1982 was a very poor year for the company—as noted previously, the first operating loss in Zefco's history.

The CEO said, "I must admit that you (the marketing manager) are right in stating that the move into the new plant could have been better timed and has been a drain on profitability, but I am also convinced that in the long run the decision will prove to be judicious. We were nearly operating at full capacity at the other plants, and a move was an inevitability. Besides, although you were not aware of it, our rental rates on the old facilities were about to be raised."

The usually reticent and very-supportive-of-the-CEO vice president of engineering was now motivated to contribute to the analyses of Zefco's troubles. "Frankly, (he always begins a serious comment with that word), I believe that our problems started with the decision to diversify into the manufacturing of plastic containers. The technology was very different from the composite and metal business we were accustomed to, and our trip up the learning curve was costly." (Even more so than at first thought because much of the inventory writedown in 1984 was in plastic containers.)

Zefco's diversification into the manufacture of plastic containers began in 1981. In the midst of the most severe recession that Zefco had ever experienced, the company discovered that its traditional container business was being buffeted from two directions. First, overall industry demand for all types of containers was weak as a result of the continuing recession. And second, plastic containers were being increasingly substituted for some of the company's metal and composite containers. A number of Zefco's direct competitors were expanding their manufacturing capabilities in plastics, and several of Zefco's good customers had inquired about Zefco's intentions in this regard. It seemed appropriate that Zefco should become involved in plastics. The alternative seemed to be a loss of business and gradual fading into an uncompetitive position.

After a brief and apparently inadequate study, Zefco acquired two new, state-of-the-art injection/blow molder machines from one of the leading manufacturers of such equipment. The total cost of acquiring and installing the machinery and related equipment was $600,000. The set-up in the new facility was completed in December, 1981, but the start-up was not commenced until January, 1982.

Although Zefco's bank was quite interested in financing 80 percent of the purchase with a five-year term loan (with Zefco anteing-up the other 20 percent), another alternative was selected—leasing. This option gave Zefco 100 percent financing over seven years and, because it was able to trade its investment tax credit on the purchase to the lessor, the interest factor was lower. In addition, the payment stream was as at a fixed rate unlike the bank's proposal with its floating interest rate.

As 1982 began, Zefco was poised for a return to rapid growth in sales. Unfortunately, the economy was still mired in an environment of high interest rates, intense competition and a declining real rate of economic growth. Despite increased capacity and an expanded product line, Zefco's sales actually declined slightly in 1982. Adding to the company's troubles were technical difficulties and consequent product quality problems with the new plastics manufacturing equipment. The vice presidents of engineering and operations worked long and hard to solve the problems, but they could not eliminate the inexperience factor overnight. It took most of 1982 to get the bugs out and to develop a well trained team of operators.

Besides acquiring new plant and equipment, diversifying into a new line of business also meant that new raw materials and other suppliers would be needed. Most vendors were all too happy to offer Zefco trade credit—the company's payment history had been impeccable.

The CEO knew that he had to agree with his loyal and trusted engineering manager, but before he had the chance to thank him for his contributions, the accounting manager (buoyed by the acknowledgments that the problems were broader and deeper than weak accounting and controls) said, "I concur with the previous observations and I'd like to add to them."

The CEO nodded approvingly.

"The new product lines we introduced meant that Zefco also needed to expand its inventory and, with the additional capacity, it needed to find more customers. Based on what the outside auditors have found, Zefco didn't do a good job of managing its inventory or evaluating the creditworthiness of some of its new customers."

"And whose responsibility is that?" the marketing manager asked.

"In part," answered the accounting manager, "my predecessors and others of us in the finance department were at fault, but your department was also responsible."

"You're crazy, all we do is sell the stuff."

"Well, you obviously didn't do a very good job of it," fired back the finance manager. "If you hadn't insisted on building inventory, expanding product lines, reducing prices, and recommending new, marginally creditworthy customers from areas outside Zefco's traditional marketing territory, we might have had better luck in establishing controls. All you marketing types ever think about is making a sale. You guys have to realize that a sale is not a sale until the money is in the till!"

"How profound!" the marketing manager responded.

Before the argument could deteriorate into something unpleasant, the CEO said "Let's take a break."

After 20 minutes, tempers cooled down and the meeting resumed.

The CEO began by saying, "You know, after listening to us argue about this problem for the past several hours, I think that we're all being extremely defensive and protective of our own turf. Let's try to be a little more objective." With that admonishment the Zefco managers resumed the analysis of the problem.

"You're right." the personnel manager said. "I've been thinking about my department's contribution to the Zefco problems. Our company has been very generous to its employees, and it has usually maintained a workforce at higher than needed levels to take advantage of opportunities when recessions turn to growth phases. Additionally, our perquisites for managers have typically been much better than our competitors. (Nearly everyone cringed at that observation.) As you all know, I have been a strong supporter of that strategy; a dedicated and loyal workforce is a productive one. Zefco's personnel policies have always followed that concept. Given the facts that have surfaced in the past week or so, maybe it's time to rethink that position."

"Folks," said the CEO, "I think we've addressed the causes of Zefco's problems enough. I'm now convinced that we, all of us in this room, must accept the burden for the company's current financial crisis. We've made, I think, honest but nevertheless serious mistakes in managing Zefco. I'm not sure what price we'll have to pay as individuals, but I do know we have got to be completely honest with ourselves, our employees, our bankers and our other creditors if we're going to solve the problem.

"What I'd like to know now," the CEO continued, "is the nature of Zefco's problems. Are they continuing to grow? Can we take prompt remedial action to correct some or all of them? And how well informed are our employees, our creditors and our customers about the seriousness of the company's cash flow problems? I want to get together again next week after my meeting with the bank, to begin developing a new strategic plan. And I want each of you to begin thinking about measures we can take to get this company turned around."

The next day, Sunday, after what would become the first of many restless nights of sleep, the CEO began to develop an outline for his meeting with the bank officers who had summoned him to their offices. The CEO listed the primary causes of Zefco's financial problems as follows:

- The severe and protracted recession
- Inadequate internal financial and accounting controls
- Failure to follow recommendations of outside CPAs
- The ill-timed acquisition of Winco
- Expansion into new markets with little planning
- Pursuit of additional customers by relaxing credit standards
- Diversification into new product lines
- The high cost of the move to new, larger facilities
- Maintenance of a higher-than-required workforce
- Capitalization of labor costs that should have been expensed
- Reluctance to hold prices of products at profitable levels to retain or gain market share

- Financing virtually all expansion and diversification with borrowed funds and
- Using working capital to finance fixed assets.

The CEO began to feel comfortable about his grasp of the causes of Zefco's troubles, but he still did not have a complete understanding of the seriousness and the magnitude of the financial problems. In the next few days, though, he would find out.

The meeting with the bank's officers began, as always, cordially. The CEO was given the opportunity to give a full and complete presentation of the causes of Zefco's financial problems. The bank officers listened intently and took copious notes. After Zefco's CEO had finished his presentation, the bank's senior credit administrator in the region said, "We greatly appreciate your thorough explanation of the problems. We believe that the mistakes made were honest ones, and we want to help you overcome these financial setbacks, but please understand, we are not going to continue funding Zefco beyond next Monday unless we have a more complete picture of the company's current and prospective financial position. We would like to see a detailed cash flow forecast for Zefco covering the next 12 months."

The CEO had not expected to be received with open arms, but he hadn't anticipated being met with such bluntness either. After all, Zefco had been a good and profitable customer of the bank for over 25 years and had never caused the bank any problems. In fact, the company had referred business to the bank.

"I don't think I quite understand," the CEO said.

"Given the financial facts which have recently come to light," the credit officer responded, "we think Zefco's viability is extremely tenuous. We're very concerned about what your other creditors are going to do. We think Zefco is in an overloan position. We're working on the formula right now. If you eliminate the goodwill account on your company's balance sheet, it has a deficit tangible net worth. Zefco could be on its way to becoming a failed business, and we don't want to have good money chasing bad money. In short, the bank is concerned about the collectibility of its loans to Zefco. I can't make myself any clearer than that."

Indeed, he couldn't. Although there was more to come, Zefco's CEO had just received the biggest shock in his business life.

The bank officials spent the next several minutes reassuring Zefco's CEO that the bank would help in any responsible, prudent and reasonable manner it could. (In substance, it meant that significant financial improvements would be necessary in the near future.) As the meeting drew to a close, the credit officer suggested that it might be in the company's best interests to retain a specialized business advisor to help prepare the financial forecasts requested. He gave the CEO the names and telephone numbers of three such consultants.

The CEO returned to Zefco's offices physically and emotionally spent. His world was suddenly crumbling around him, and there seemed no way to reverse matters.

"At least," he thought to himself as he entered his panelled office, "it can't get any worse than this."

Of course he was mistaken. It could and would get worse before getting better.

He briefed his lieutenants about his meeting with the bank. They all seemed resigned to the worst but promised to keep a stiff upper lip while the business followed whatever course was available to it. The CEO decided to call one of the consultants that had been recommended by the bank. In the meantime, he exhorted his managers to think about ways to improve things in each of their departments.

Chapter

3

Zefco's Decision to Retain
a Turnaround Consultant

Late in the afternoon, following his consciousness-raising meeting with Zefco's bankers, and his debriefing session with the company's key managers, the CEO placed a call to one of the three business consultants who had been recommended by the bank. Lenders often offer the names of more than one person or firm from whom a troubled borrower can choose. They do so in order to suggest rather than to direct the action to be taken. There are potentially very powerful legal implications and financial ramifications in how this situation is handled.

Despite the bank's admonition to interview more than one prospective advisor, the CEO decided to proceed with the first consultant he contacted. It is not unusual for this to happen. Businesses in trouble react quickly and without careful evaluation. Sometimes this compounds the problem instead of leading to an earlier solution.

After a quick introduction, the CEO began, "My company recently incurred a substantial net operating loss, and our bank suggested that someone such as yourself might be able to help with pushing the numbers. Could we meet at my office and possibly begin working together early tomorrow morning—I've got to have a 12-month cash flow forecast by next week, or the bank might stop financing Zefco and possibly call its loans."

The consultant, who had previously worked with scores of other similarly anxious and apparently distraught business managers and owners, said, "The time and place for the meeting are fine." (In fact, he felt it was always best to start critical meetings as early in the day as practicable.) "But first let me ask you to have your accounting staff pull together some financial data."

"All right," the CEO responded, "what do you need?"

The consultant stated, "*We* [emphasis added] need to review several management reports. First, we want to know the current balance of Zefco's checking account—not the balance that shows on the bank's books for the company but the balance that would appear if all the checks that have been written and issued were presented for payment to the bank concurrently."

The consultant knows from experience that Zefco's checkbook balance will probably be negative—it almost always is for businesses experiencing serious financial difficulties.

The business advisor requested the additional list of information:

• Monthly agings of accounts receivable and accounts payable for the past year
• A current list of inventory
• A detailed schedule of fixed assets
• A copy of the loan and security agreement with the bank
• Detailed schedules of notes payable and other long-term debt
• Detailed schedules of current costs and expenses
• Copies of Zefco's corporate tax returns for the past three years
• A recent copy of the CEO's personal financial statement, and
• Zefco's annual financial statements for the past five years.

"Are you sure that's all the information you want," the CEO said somewhat sarcastically.

"That should do for a start," the consultant replied. "We're going to review the data pretty intensively tomorrow to try and get a handle on how pressing the problems really are."

From the CEO's response to the preliminary questioning and

request for information, the prospective advisor to Zefco surmised that the CEO was not completely familiar with these financial data.

"Oh, there is one more thing," the consultant added. "Get yourself a notebook. Before we're finished, you'll probably fill it up."

"Should I ask the other members of my management team to join us at tomorrow morning's meeting?" the CEO asked.

"Not just yet," the consultant said. "But we'll definitely want their input in the next few weeks."

The next morning, the business consultant arrived at Zefco's corporate offices promptly at 8 A.M. (Consultants are never allowed to be late.)

"Before starting our discussion about Zefco's troubles," the consultant said, "please let me explain a little bit about myself and my background."

The business advisor gave the CEO a brief history of himself and a copy of his brochure that included his professional experiences and academic qualifications, the various types of consulting assignments completed, and a list of references.

It is extremely important for prospective clients of consultants to know as much as possible about them. Financial crises make managers more vulnerable to suggestions—especially those that promise a relief from mounting day-to-day pressures. The fact that a particular outside consultant has been recommended by a banker, an accountant, a member of management, a lawyer or a director is a strong but not a sufficient reason for retaining him or her.

Good chemistry between the CEO and the consultant is vitally important. If the initial fit is not good, and this can be determined in a few hours of conversation, seek other recommendations. Don't make the mistake of retaining someone with whom you intuitively suspect you won't be satisfied. Your banker or other major creditors will go to great lengths to ensure that you are not forced to accept any one turnaround consultant—they are sensitive about becoming directly involved in the management of your business.

"Well, sir," the CEO said, "I appreciate your advice on that subject. Although I know the bank wouldn't recommend you if you weren't capable, I will do as you suggest and check with some of your former clients and other references.

"Before we begin crunching numbers," the CEO continued, "can you give me a general idea of how much your services are going to cost and if Zefco must pay for all of them."

This is an excellent question and should be asked and answered early in the initial meeting between the CEO and prospective advisor. One thing is nearly universally true for financially troubled businesses—they, not the creditors, are responsible for paying for such professional services.

The business consultant responded, "My total fee will be directly related to how much time and energy you are personally willing to invest in this turnaround effort. For example, a lot of different financial scenarios may be requested by the bank and other creditors as we go forward. If you own or have access to a personal computer, and you know how to use a spreadsheet software program, you will be able to do the work as well as develop a better understanding and control of what is occurring in your company on a daily basis.

"In other words, the more pro-actively you become involved in the process the less you will need me or other outside professionals. To answer your question about cost more directly though, my fee for services rendered is computed at the rate of $150 per hour. An initial retainer of $4,500 is required and when, or if, that amount is depleted additional retainers will be requested in multiples of $3,000.

"To summarize, depending on your leadership role in the turnaround and the difficulties we experience with the various classes of creditors, my total fee will vary between about $9,000 and $45,000."

The CEO thought to himself, "That's outrageous!" but he managed to restrain from saying so. He assumed there was no alternative.

"How long do you think it will take to turn Zefco around?" the CEO asked.

The consultant answered, "In the range of two to four months all of the parties-in-interest should have a pretty good idea about what most of the possible solutions to Zefco's financial troubles will be. The solution to the problem could take as long as a few additional months to as much as several years, depending upon the route selected. But we're getting ahead of ourselves. Let's start talking about the cash flow forecast that the bank wants to see by next week."

"What is so magical about a cash flow forecast," asked the CEO, "and why does the bank feel it is so necessary to have one in the next week?"

The consultant responded "The bank's credit officer believes, and I concur with him 100 percent, that a cash flow forecast is the most critical financial or management report that your company will be producing for at least the next several months. The value of this report is that it shows where the cash will be coming from and where it will be going. It is a pure flow of funds.

"Cash is the the life's blood of all businesses; it becomes especially critical if it's not available from external sources. Since the bank is likely to remain Zefco's primary conduit of cash flow, it wants to be sure that your company uses its cash in the most judicious manner possible. The bank doesn't want Zefco to use its money to pay previously incurred debt. The bank also wants to know if Zefco will require (but frankly hoping it won't) additional funding.

"Furthermore, cash flow forecasts allow the reviewers of such reports to strip away the effects of accrual accounting. I call this 'checkbook accounting' because, all other things being equal, if you have more cash in your checking account at the end of the month than you had at the beginning of the month, you probably had a positive cash flow from operations in that period. This will become clearer as we go forward. Okay, let's create a cash flow statement for Zefco.

"In our first iteration, we are going to present the Worst Case Scenario—this assumes that sales decline from current levels by, say, 10 percent while costs and expenses remain at their current rates."

"But why do we want to assume the worst case?" the CEO asked. "We're expecting 1985 to be a very strong year for sales. Won't this paint a worse picture than is likely to occur? And mightn't that further hurt our position with the bank and other creditors?"

"Perhaps," answered the business consultant, " but there are seldom any penalties associated with exceeding financial forecasts with which creditors are in agreement. The problems will arise if Zefco misses the mark on the down side. One of our primary objectives is to assume the worst and plan for the best."

"Let's get started on the numbers," the consultant said, as he removed some forms from his briefcase. Following his conversation with the CEO the previous evening, the business advisor had prepared the basic outline for creating cash flow statements for Zefco. The uncompleted forms are shown below in Table 3-1, Table 3-2 and Table 3-3.

"I realize," the consultant said to the CEO, "that you probably won't be able instantly to complete the forms by yourself, but with assistance from your accounting staff and a little coaching from me, you should very quickly develop the necessary skills. And you'll be amazed at how simple it is to update and use this management report."

"Have you got Zefco's current checkbook balance handy?" the advisor continued.

The CEO responded with a faintly furrowed brow, "My accounting manager told me this morning that the book balance in Zefco's checking account is a negative $73,852. However, of that amount, approximately $47,000 has not yet been released to vendors, and the balance represents float—per the bank's books, Zefco has a positive balance of almost $3,000."

"I was afraid that would be the case," the business consultant said. "You can no longer permit Zefco to operate with a deficit checkbook balance. You can't take a chance of bouncing a check. I'd suggest you have two things done immediately. First, tear up and throw away the $47,000 in internally-held checks; and second, eliminate payments to trade vendors until you achieve a positive checkbook balance."

"We can't do those things—at least not that fast." the CEO countered. "Our purchasing manager told me that he has given certain vendors his promise that payment would be made on materials. In addition, some critically important suppliers won't ship or deliver unless Zefco pays on a COD basis or with a cashier's check. We've been receiving some shipments on credit and we've already started using the materials. Look, his reputation is on the line. For that matter, so is mine because I backed him up."

TABLE 3-1

Zefco Container Mfg. Co., Inc.
Cash Flow Forecast—Collections
For the Twelve Months Ending
March 31, 1986
(in thousands of dollars)

	Apr	May	Jun	Jul	Aug	Sep	Oct	Nov	Dec	Jan	Feb	Mar	Total
Net sales estimates													
Collection of existing accounts receivable:													
Prior to January													
From January sales													
From February sales													
From March Sales													
Subtotal													
Collection of future accounts receivable:													
April Sales													
May Sales													
June sales													
July sales													
August Sales													
September sales													
October sales													
November sales													
December sales													
January sales													
February sales													
March sales													
Subtotal													
Collection of tax refund													
Total collections													

TABLE 3–2

Cash Flow Forecast—Cash Disbursements for the Twelve Months Ending March 31, 1986
(in thousands of dollars)

Cash disbursements:	Apr	May	Jun	Jul	Aug	Sep	Oct	Nov	Dec	Jan	Feb	Mar	Total
For operations:													
Purchases													
Wages, salaries, benefits, and payroll taxes													
Rent on building													
Repairs and maintenance													
Telephone and utilities													
Insurance													
Truck operating expenses													
Auto operating expenses													
Rent on office equipment													
Office expenses													
Professional services													
Travel and entertainment													
Taxes and licenses													
Miscellaneous mfg. exp.													
Dues and subscriptions													
Other expenses													
Subtotal													
For servicing debt:													
Interest:													
Bank													
Others													
Principal:													
Bank													
Others													
Leases:													
Mfg. equipment													
Vehicles													
Subtotal													
For reducing prior payables and accruals													
For overdraft at bank													
Total cash disbursements													

TABLE 3–3

Cash Flow Forecast—Flow of Funds for the Twelve Months Ending March 31, 1986
(in thousands of dollars)

	Apr	May	Jun	Jul	Aug	Sep	Oct	Nov	Dec	Jan	Feb	Mar	Total
Cash or (deficit) at beginning of period													
Accounts receivable at beginning of period													
Net sales													
Collections*													
Accounts receivable at end of period													
Less: ineligible accounts receivable													
Eligible accounts receivable													
Available from bank at 80%													
Inventory at end of period													
Available from bank at 30%													
Total revolving loan available (A/R plus inventory)													
Revolving loan balance at beginning of period													
Cash disbursements**													
Collections*													
Revolving loan balance at end of period													
Availability or (overloan) at end of period													

* See Table 3–1
** See Table 3–2

"I really do understand and appreciate the dilemma you face as well as the humiliation and embarrassment this will cause for you and your purchasing manager," the consultant said as consolingly as he could, "but let me remind you of what you told me when you called yesterday—the bank is actively considering the possibility that it will cease financing Zefco next week. If it does take that action, it certainly will not pay any items if your company's checking account is in an NSF (insufficient funds) position. Believe me, Zefco will fare much better in the weeks ahead if it does not bounce any checks."

With reluctance the CEO conceded the point. "All right," he said, "I'll talk to my people about this matter as soon as we're finished here."

"This might be a good time to start using the notebook I suggested you get," the consultant said.

"Dammit!" the CEO exclaimed, "I forgot to pick one up last night." (Regrettably, harsh invectives, profanities and vulgarisms do slip into use as tensions rise, but we will try to keep a civil pen.)

"No problem," the financial advisor replied as he reached into his briefcase and withdrew a new, spiral bound notebook having about 80 lined, blank pages. "I always carry a spare."

As he handed it across the desk to the CEO he said, "This will become a very important reference document, and you should plan to carry it in your briefcase wherever you go.

"There are three parts to the notebook:

an 'Action Steps' section;
a 'Synopsis of Meetings' section; and
an 'Important Contacts' section.

"In the first section, each separate action step should be given a due date, a responsibility assignment and a completion date. The synopsis of meetings is self-explanatory. The section on important contacts should include office telephone numbers and home telephone numbers if obtainable. Successful turnarounds require occasional contacts with key decision-makers at night and on weekends. The next month or two could have a number of seven-day workweeks.

"The first action step you might want to list is 'Eliminate

checkbook overdraft position.' I'd also suggest that you person-ally make sure it's done."

"What's next on the agenda?" the CEO inquired somewhat impatiently.

Sensing that a break was needed, the consultant answered, "If you don't mind I'd like to spend an hour or so studying the other documents we've had assembled. Is there a room I could use?"

"Sure," the CEO responded, "use the conference room down the hall. It has a telephone if you need one."

As the advisor ensconced himself in the conference room to peruse the financial data, the CEO reflected on this initial meet-ing with the consultant. He was not entirely comfortable with the constant emphasis on financial matters, and he had a nagging feeling that the consultant wasn't going to be a member of the "Zefco team." However, he also realized that he would need help in restoring credibility with the bank.

Shortly thereafter he placed a call to the credit officer he had recently met at the bank. He said to his new banker, "I've decided to retain one of the consultants the bank has recommended. We should have the cash flow statement ready to show you next Monday."

After a brief exchange of pleasantries, the credit officer replied cryptically, "Very well, I look forward to seeing you fellows and taking a hard look at the data. Sorry to rush you but I've got to run off to another meeting." (Credit officers specializ-ing in problem loans often have 10 or more borrowers in the loan portfolios under their supervision. In fact, day-after-day crisis meetings are a way of life for this special breed of bankers. Quite often they need to cut conversations short and go tackle another problem.)

Although the phone call was brought to a close faster than he would have liked, the CEO felt that he had struck a good chord with the banker by reacting quickly to his suggestion that Zefco seek financial advice from an independent source.

The consultant finished his analysis in less time than he had expected and returned to the CEO's office. "Are you ready to resume?" he asked the CEO.

"Yes," came the reply. "Let's go."

The consultant began with the following question, "Do you understand why I am using this format [shown in Table 3–3] to present the flow of funds of the cash flow forecast." The CEO gestured that he did not.

"I'm using it because, for an indeterminate period, I think it is very, very likely that Zefco will be at the mercy of the bank for providing all of the financing necessary to operate the company. The bank credit people are, or will soon be, on the horns of a dilemma. Since Zefco's financial ratios have deteriorated so badly and so quickly, the company isn't really 'bankable' right now; yet, because Zefco's financial future is so uncertain, it is extremely improbable that even an aggressive asset-based lender would be interested in refinancing Zefco's loans at your bank. In short, the bank no longer wants Zefco as a customer, but it knows that it can't realistically expect the company to find another home—at least not right now. It's either turn around or belly up."

"I'm terribly confused and upset by those comments," the CEO said. "How do you know that the bank is thinking along those lines? I've had good rapport with some of the senior officers of that bank for many years. In fact, six months ago I was invited to a luncheon at the bank's executive dining room and told how much they appreciated Zefco's business. Although my meeting with the bank yesterday was anything but pleasant, I didn't get the slightest inkling that they really want to get rid of Zefco as a customer or that they think the company is about to go bust."

Without hesitation the consultant answered, "I've worked with a good many businesses which have experienced financial setbacks similar to Zefco's, and the path each has followed has been roughly the same. The outside bank regulators and the bank's internal loan review department strongly influence the disposition of problem loans. In my professional opinion, Zefco's current financial profile will very shortly make it a candidate for official criticism. When that occurs the options available to the bank officers managing your account will become fewer and less flexible. My experience with lenders, in general, and the credit man at your bank in particular, tells me that we've got to move quickly if we're going to keep the initiative.

"One of the toughest things you're going to have to do, and do quickly as the point man in this turnaround, is develop a mindset that parallels your creditors. They want their money back from Zefco *now*, and they really don't want to hear sob stories or other rationalizations. Your dilemma is to assure them that a repayment plan is on the way—and ultimately is delivered—while retaining sufficient funds to operate the business. And I can help you learn the ropes. I apologize for being so blunt, but I consider it my primary obligation to be completely candid with you. We've got to confront difficult issues head-on because time is not our ally.

"I suspect you're finding some of my statements somewhat incredulous but, remember my words, very soon the rest of Zefco's creditors are going to comprehend what's happened to the company, and they're going to want to see a repayment program of some kind."

"Well, I am very surprised that you could reach the conclusions you did so quickly," the CEO said. "If you're correct, you're making me feel terribly inadequate. Are Zefco's problems really that bad and so obvious?"

The consultant nodded affirmatively.

"You make it seem as though the company is plunging toward financial ruin," the CEO continued. "Maybe we should file for protection under Chapter 11 of the U.S. Bankruptcy Code."

The consultant said, "I wouldn't rule that action out down the road. It's quite possible that Zefco might need to seek legal protection from creditor lawsuits as a means of effecting a turnaround (plan of reorganization). But using the courts is an option I feel should be avoided unless it becomes absolutely necessary. But you're right. Inaction or inappropriate action on our part could mandate our use of that alternative."

Adopting points of reference that are very similar to those of creditors runs counter to the ideas of most entreprenuerially driven owners and managers of small and medium-sized businesses—especially those experiencing severe financial adversity. Accordingly, many such owners and managers have great difficulty in making the shift in their thinking. Nevertheless, if survival of the business is the paramount objective—which it should be—then the question is not whether such changes in perspective should be made but rather, when and under whose direction—the debtor's or the creditors'.

Experience in turnaround management indicates that there are about two to eight weeks between the announcement of an extremely serious financial problem, like Zefco's, and the creditors' independent decisions to seek repayment of their debts through threatened or real legal actions, which frequently result in the filing of a bankruptcy petition.

During the recognition and adjustment period, decisive actions can be taken to achieve a successful turnaround without the aid of the bankruptcy court. If done expeditiously, but carefully, a business can maintain control of the situation as well as restore the confidence of its creditors.

The CEO said, "I'm beginning to get the picture that you think things are seriously off center at Zefco. For the moment, at least, I'm willing to defer to your reasoning. I've got to believe that you wouldn't make those Armagedden-like comments if you weren't pretty confident about your analysis of the situation—particularly since I haven't paid you anything yet. Okay," he chuckled, "let's continue the grilling."

"What are the chances of your being able to put some more of your own money into Zefco?" the consultant asked.

"You saw my personal financial statement," the CEO answered. "I don't have anything else to contribute. The fact is if Zefco fails, I'll probably lose my shirt as well because I've personally guaranteed and secured the company's debts to the bank."

Continuing his probing, the consultant said, "Tell me what you think are all of the sources of cash available to Zefco during the next year or so."

"That's a pretty tough question," the CEO replied. "It's not really in my bailiwick but I'll give it a try. Well, I suppose Zefco won't be having any public offerings of common stock or bonds," he grinned. "It's worth confirming, but I'm also sure that all of the company's assets are already pledged to the bank or other secured creditors, so Zefco probably can't raise new money from those sources. Oh, I know, we could possibly sell some machinery and equipment that we're not using right now."

"But," asked the consultant, "won't the liens of secured creditors have to be satisfied?"

"You're right," the CEO answered, "we won't get much if anything there either. Ah, of course," the CEO said after a moment's reflection, "collections of accounts receivable. That's where we get most of our cash."

"What percentage of Zefco's collections does the company get to retain?" the consultant asked.

"I'm not sure," the CEO answered. "It's 100 percent, isn't it?"

"Not likely," the advisor said. "If it's structured like most revolving accounts receivable lines of credit, Zefco has probably been obtaining 20 percent of its collections and 80 percent of its newly invoiced sales. The effect appears to be the same, but as you will see in going through this exercise a few times, it is quite different when sales are declining rather than advancing."

"That's the second time you've mentioned sales going down," the CEO said with a touch of renewed anger. "I've already mentioned that the sales outlook for Zefco is bullish if anything. Lower sales just aren't in the cards in my opinion. Let's talk about this."

"Good, tell me how you are going to finance Zefco's growth in sales," the consultant said. "Your creditors aren't going to want to *lend* the company more funds or materials; they'll want Zefco to *repay* some of the credit previously extended."

The CEO responded, "Are you saying that if Zefco has a valid purchase order for good business, the company won't get temporary credit to fill the order?"

"Absolutely!" came the reply. "Who wants to give additional unsecured credit to a business that's just had a $491,000 net operating loss? Is the goal Zefco is chasing sales or bottom line profits? I believe Zefco will be required to pay COD, or even cash before delivery, for nearly all purchases of goods and services. In other words, no creditor is likely to be interested in financing any more Zefco losses. Before sales volume can again grow with external funds, demonstrable evidence of profitability is needed.

"Also, a certain number of your customers will simply stop doing business with Zefco when they learn of its problems. They won't risk an interruption in their sources of supply. Let me level with you, instead of thinking business expansion, you've got to accept business contraction; instead of seeking additional borrowings you've got think debt shrinkage."

"You really know how to let the air out of a person's balloon, don't you?" the CEO said and sighed resignedly.

"Believe me," the advisor said, "my only interest is in helping you in your efforts at revitalizing Zefco and renewing its successful operation."

"This discussion has left me mentally exhausted," the CEO said. "Do you mind if we call it a day. I'd like to think some more about what you've said and clear out a few of the cobwebs. I certainly was not prepared for a meeting of this type. I thought we'd grind out a few numbers and go from there. I do want you to know, though, that I appreciate your frank approach to Zefco's financial troubles. Also, I've decided to retain your services to help the company achieve a turnaround."

With that the CEO called the accounting manager and instructed him to issue a check in the amount of $4,500 to the business consultant.

"Before leaving," the advisor said, "I want you to know that if, at any time in the future, you decide I'm not performing up to your expectations you can fire me, no questions asked and no hurt feelings. By the same token if I find evidence of impropriety or dishonesty I will resign from this engagement if you or associates try to stonewall the matter.

"I'll refund any unused portion of the retainer and give you a full accounting of my services up to that point. I want our relationship to be 'win-win' at all times. I'll see you tomorrow afternoon at 1:30. I need to study the financial data before we develop the first iteration of the cash flow forecast." He then trundled off with the box of financial reports.

Successful out-of-court turnarounds require that the debtor, the creditors and other parties-in-interest adhere to a rigid code of ethics built upon absolute honesty and integrity. The fragility of a reorganization outside the Bankruptcy court is so great that even a perceived breach of faith can snowball into a failed business. Promises should never be made, but if they are, they must be kept.

Is it really necessary for a business in trouble to retain an outside turnaround specialist as Zefco has done? It most decidedly is *not* a requirement that a consultant be brought in to turn around an ailing company. Understanding and implementing the process of achieving a business turnaround is well within the grasp of most managers if they are willing to face up to the difficult decisions that must be made.

Actually, there are only five major steps needed to begin a successful turnaround program and all of them can be completed within a three to six month period. They are:

- The preparation of a clearly articulated, written analysis of the causes and the nature of the financial difficulties (What happened?)
- The creation of a cash flow statement that shows the financial problems with which the business must deal (What's happening now?)
- The development of a new, written strategic plan based on the precariousness of the financial condition of the company (What's going to happen?)
- Meetings with various classes of creditors to explain the three previous steps the business is taking to achieve a turnaround and to ask for their support and forebearance
- The preparation of a Plan of Reorganization and a Disclosure Statement which formally document the proposed turnaround.

The principal advantage of using an outside turnaround consultant is that such a person is experienced in knowing what needs to be done, when it needs to be accomplished, and how to do it. But all of those things can be learned. It is a matter of how much time the owners and managers of the affected business have before the creditors lose all confidence.

I am convinced that if the reader carefully follows the steps outlined in the remainder of this book he or she will be able to deal much more effectively with the stresses of a turnaround. Perhaps the biggest problem a manager faces is dealing with the unknown. This book will help you to demystify the world of turnarounds.

Chapter

4

Preparing Cash Flow Forecasts

The newly retained business consultant spent the next morning analyzing Zefco's numbers more thoroughly. His first step was to review the aging of accounts receivable and accounts payable for the past 12 months. This exercise has a dual purpose: first, to determine if Zefco might be able to accelerate collections and/or slow down disbursements in order to increase the flow of funds on a short-term basis and build liquidity; and second, to determine how seriously accessibility to trade credit had been impaired. The summarized data are shown in Table 4–1.

It is fairly common for a financially troubled business to have a poorly managed credit and collections department. One expects to see the average collection period of accounts receivable to be well below industry norms. (Robert Morris Associates, based in Philadelphia, Pennsylvania, is a leading compiler of industry data such as these.) Additionally, documentation of credit sales is usually inadequate, and there is a lack of credit profiles on accounts.

In Zefco's case, however, the numbers are not as bad as might have been expected. The collection period between March, 1984, and November, 1984, varied between 37 and 40 days. After the

TABLE 4-1

Zefco Container Mfg. Co., Inc.
Summary Agings of Accounts Receivable and Accounts Payable for the Period March 1984 to February 1985

	Mar	Apr	May	Jun	Jul	Aug	Sep	Oct	Nov	Dec	Jan	Feb
Accounts receivable:												
In thousands of dollars												
Current	347	352	355	358	360	370	378	386	394	368	375	390
Over 30 days	71	66	67	71	72	71	74	76	74	72	75	78
Over 60 days	30	38	41	42	45	46	47	51	52	34	40	39
Over 90 days	12	14	17	19	23	23	26	27	30	10	10	13
Total	460	470	480	490	500	510	525	540	550	490	500	520
In percent												
Current	75.5	75.0	74.0	73.0	72.0	72.5	72.0	71.5	71.5	75.0	75.0	75.0
Over 30 days	15.5	14.0	14.0	14.5	14.5	14.0	14.0	14.0	13.5	16.0	15.0	15.0
Over 60 days	6.5	8.0	8.5	8.5	9.0	9.0	9.0	9.5	9.5	7.0	8.0	7.5
Over 90 days	2.5	3.0	3.5	4.0	4.5	4.5	5.0	5.0	5.5	2.0	2.0	2.5
Total	100.0	100.0	100.0	100.0	100.0	100.0	100.0	100.0	100.0	100.0	100.0	100.0
Number of customers	125	126	128	129	130	131	133	134	136	137	132	132
Accounts payable:												
In thousands of dollars												
Current	114	118	115	116	113	109	111	108	109	110	108	104
Over 30 days	304	290	290	288	290	279	258	241	223	204	193	178
Over 60 days	304	330	338	344	346	365	385	407	428	451	473	496
Over 90 days	38	47	52	52	56	57	66	74	80	85	86	92
Total	760	785	795	800	805	810	820	830	840	850	860	870
In percent												
Current	15.0	15.0	14.5	14.5	14.0	13.5	13.5	13.0	13.0	13.0	12.5	12.0
Over 30 days	40.0	37.0	36.5	36.0	36.0	34.5	31.5	29.0	26.5	24.0	22.5	20.5
Over 60 days	40.0	42.0	42.5	43.0	43.0	45.0	47.0	49.0	51.0	53.0	55.0	57.0
Over 90 days	5.0	6.0	6.5	6.5	7.0	7.0	8.0	9.0	9.5	10.0	10.0	10.5
Total	100.0	100.0	100.0	100.0	100.0	100.0	100.0	100.0	100.0	100.0	100.0	100.0
Number of vendors	70	74	78	80	82	84	86	87	90	91	96	97

year-end adjustments required by the outside auditors, the collection period was lowered to 35 days. As shown previously in Table 1–3, the pattern has been remarkably stable over the past three years.

It appears that Zefco's credit manager had performed quite well on behalf of his employer despite the write-offs taken at the end of 1984. The consultant later found out that the credit manager had 25 years of experience with Zefco and had argued against giving credit to customers with spotty financial records but had been overruled. The business advisor was not enthusiastic at seeing these statistics because he knew that little substantive improvement could be made in this area of cash flow management.

Accounts payable, on the other hand, were much worse than he would have liked to see. Three problems virtually leapt from the spreadsheet containing the summary agings of accounts payable. First, total accounts payable increased by $110,000, or 14.5 percent, on a year-over-year basis. Second, the combined "over 60" and "over 90" categories had deteriorated badly from 45.0 percent to 67.5 percent of the total accounts payable. And third, the number of vendors had increased from 70 to 97, or 38.6 percent, in one year.

The situation had the look of a time bomb ready to explode. As soon as Zefco vendors realized that Zefco was on the brink of insolvency, all trade credit would abruptly cease, and the incessant phone calls from angry creditors would start. The worst-case scenario of the cash-flow forecast would need to reflect some program to reverse this condition.

The consultant needed one additional set of data before meeting with Zefco's CEO and starting work on the cash flow forecast—how long does it take for Zefco to collect on its credit sales? In other words, if the company's sales for April, 1985, are $450,000 over what period of time will it take to collect the funds?

After delving into the detailed monthly accounts-receivable agings, the business advisor found that collections typically occurred in the following pattern: 99 percent of all credit sales are ultimately collected; 17 percent of all collections of credit sales for the average month are received in the same month (reflecting certain customers' interests in taking advantage of Zefco's 2/10 net 30 day discount policy); 60 percent are received within 31 to 60 days; 13 percent within 61 to 90 days; 7 percent within the 91 to 120 day period; and 3 percent within 121 to 150 days. The consultant was ready to begin.

That afternoon the CEO and the consultant met to begin working on the cash flow forecast—worst case scenario.

"Ready to start?" the consultant asked.

"I'm champing at the bit," the CEO responded. "Let's get moving."

"What will sales be over the next 12 months?" the advisor asked.

"Well, we're now doing about $450,000 a month with practically no seasonality. We could go to $500,000 per month by year end, but using your worst case scenario, the current figure should drop by 10 percent to $405,000 a month. That's $4,860,000 on an annualized basis, if my math's right. About the same as last year."

"Okay, I think that's a good starting point," the consultant said, "but let's assume a gradual phase-down, say $450,000 in April, $430,000 in May, $415,000 in June and then $405,000 for the following nine months. That means sales for the next 12 months will be, let's see, $4,940,000 or thereabouts. Do you agree?"

"I still don't like it, but I guess I have to accept it," the CEO said.

"It's not immutable," the consultant replied a little testily. "It's a beginning." After a pause, he said, "Let's talk about collections. How long do you think it will take for Zefco to collect the $518,000 it has in trade accounts receivable?"

"I really don't have the foggiest notion," the CEO said, "but I'll bet you have a good idea, or you wouldn't have asked the question."

"You're right," the consultant said, "I think I do have a basis for a reasonable estimate of the timing of the collections."

He proceeded to tell the CEO about the collection pattern he had found in his analysis of the detailed agings of accounts receivable.

"If the historical collection pattern holds, Zefco will receive $513,000 of the $518,000 it is owed approximately as follows:

$345,000 in April; $106,000 in May; $47,000 in June; and $15,000 in July. That takes care of current accounts receivable collections. Now let's move on to future collections.

"April sales (all of which are on credit) are forecast to be $450,000," the consultant continued. "If collections ultimately equal 99 percent of credit sales, $445,0000 will be received; and, if the usual collection pattern prevails, the funds will be received as follows: $76,000 in April (17 percent); $267,000 in May (60 percent); $58,000 in June (13 percent); $31,000 in July (7 percent); and $13,000 in August (3 percent).

"This probably is a bit confusing, but bear with me for another moment. If we apply the same technique used for April to the following 11 months, you will see a matrix developing that shows total collections over the full year."

During the next hour and a half, the CEO and the consultant worked together to complete the matrix for the collection of trade accounts receivable.

Just as they were about to finish, the consultant said, "Oh, I forgot to include one very important receivable which Zefco should receive within the next month or two—a $128,000 income tax refund resulting from the application of a tax loss carryback. I assume that your CPAs have already taken care of this matter."

"I believe you're right," the CEO said, "but I'd better jot it down in my notebook to make certain. How did you come up with the figure you mentioned?"

"I checked over the Zefco corporate tax returns you provided me," the consultant answered. "After I found out that the company paid taxes in the three prior years, I simply added up the payments which should be refundable."

The results of their combined efforts to prepare the forecast collection data are shown in Table 4–2.

Total sales over the next year will be about $4,940,000; cash collected from existing accounts receivable about $513,000; and collections from future sales and the tax refund will be about $4,542,000. In summary, on a worst case basis, total funds from operations flowing into Zefco's coffers over the next 12 months will be in the range of $5,000,000.

"Before we begin preparing the disbursements part of the cash flow forecast," the consultant said, "let me repeat my earlier

TABLE 4–2

Zefco Container Mfg. Co., Inc.
Cash Flow Forecast—Worst Case Scenario
Collections for the Twelve Months Ending March 31, 1986
(in thousands of dollars)

	Apr	May	Jun	Jul	Aug	Sep	Oct	Nov	Dec	Jan	Feb	Mar	Total
Net sales estimates	450	430	415	405	405	405	405	405	405	405	405	405	4940
Collection of existing accounts receivable:													
Prior to January		7	4	2									13
From January sales	29	13											42
From February sales	55	29	13										97
From March sales	261	57	30	13									361
Subtotal	345	106	47	15									513
Collection of future accounts receivable:													
April sales	76	267	58	31	13								445
May sales		72	256	55	30	13							426
June sales			70	247	53	29	12						411
July sales				68	241	52	28	12					401
August sales					68	241	52	28	12				401
September sales						68	241	52	28	12			401
October sales							68	241	52	28	12		401
November sales								68	241	52	28	12	401
December sales									68	241	52	28	389
January sales										68	241	52	361
February sales											68	241	309
March sales												68	68
Subtotal	76	339	384	401	405	403	401	401	401	401	401	401	4414
Collection of tax refund		128											128
Total collections	421	573	431	416	405	403	401	401	401	401	401	401	5055

comment that it is highly unlikely Zefco will be able to obtain credit in the near future from any provider of materials or services, except the bank and then only under a strict program of controls. In other words, expect to pay COD for everything."

"Understood," the CEO said. "Let's get on with it."

"Purchases (including freight)," the advisor noted, "will be the single greatest consumer of Zefco's cash over the next 12 months. In analyzing the company's detailed monthly financial statements for the past year it appears to me that purchases— credit and cash—have consistently been in the range of 46 to 47 percent of sales. I think that we should use the higher figure in this go round." The CEO nodded his approval.

"The next largest category of cash expenditures will be for wages, salaries, benefits and payroll taxes. The current payroll register is probably the best source to use for forecasting these disbursements. Would you ask someone from your accounting staff to bring in that report to us?"

"Not necessary," the CEO beamed, "I keep very close tabs on that information. I get a monthly summary on all departments, and I keep the reports locked up in my desk."

"Great," said the consultant. "What's the figure?"

"$133,000 a month," the CEO replied with obvious satisfaction that he knew the answer off the top of his head. "But since sales are forecasted to decline, we'd better cut that number. Let's use $133,000 in April, $131,000 in May, $128,000 in June and $127,000 for the rest of calendar 1985. Then we'll assume a 4 percent increase across the board beginning in 1986. What's next?"

The consultant, sensing that he had struck a potentially resonant chord, said, "All right, do you want to try your hand at forecasting the remaining costs and expenses?"

"I think I would," the CEO said. "I know the building rent is fixed at $12,800 a month. The rest of the operating data we should be able to pick off the CPA-prepared schedules of 1984's profit and loss statement. Let's see, repairs and maintenance are running about $12,000 per month, but they increase slightly during the warmer summer months. Telephone and utilities are averaging $11,000 to $12,000 per month. Boy, that seems high!"

"Let's start putting the numbers down on paper," the advisor interjected. During the next three hours, the CEO and the consultant drew upon many already existing financial schedules and reports to develop the data needed to complete the cash disbursements part of the 12-month forecast. Only two areas caused any major differences of opinion for the CEO—fees for professional services and payments to vendors.

"I just can't believe that it's going to cost Zefco $112,000 for outside services in the next 12 months," the CEO said. "That's darn near an entire month's payroll for over 50 Zefco employees!"

"Believe me," the consultant replied, "the figure could jump to over $200,000 if we're unsuccessful in persuading the creditors that their best interests lie in working through this problem with us. Besides, Zefco's fees for outside professional services have been running about $30,000 a year."

"Speaking of creditors," the CEO said, "I feel we have got to make some effort at reducing Zefco's indebtedness to vendors. Let's use $20,000 a month for this forecast." The consultant decided not to argue against the idea—for the moment.

The cash disbursement part of the forecast that the two men labored over is presented in Table 4–3.

Peering at his watch, the consultant said, "It's nearly seven o'clock. Do you want to call it a day?"

"No way," the CEO answered. "I want to get to the bottom line of this worst case scenario before we leave here tonight."

"Okay," the consultant responded. "I'm all for it, but my gut feel tells me you're not going to be happy about the figures or the indicated course of actions."

"Let the chips fall where they may," came the CEO's reply. "As you've said before, I've got to recognize and face up to the problems fast or I'm not going to get Zefco moving in the right direction. Besides, I can see by quick inspection of the collections and disbursements data we produced that the company's cash flow is negative almost every month. You're right. I'll be disappointed, but I'm past the stage of being shocked. Let's continue."

The consultant said, "Let's assume, as I've probably asked you to do *ad nauseum,* that the bank is Zefco's only external source of financing. Okay?"

"That is a rhetorical question, I presume." the CEO answered.

"Unless you are or someone close to you is about to come into a substantial inheritance or windfall which you want to invest in a business that just lost nearly a half million dollars, and no one knows exactly why it happened or if the losses will continue."

"Touché," the CEO said.

"First on the agenda," the consultant continued, "is clearing up the $27,000 technical overdraft at the bank. Although Zefco is already in an overloan position as a result of the year-end inventory write-down and accounts receivable write-offs, the bank could be persuaded to advance additional funds to cover those NSF checks when it is assigned the proceeds of the tax refund. So, basically, Zefco could start off its turnaround program having a very narrow, but positive, availability to borrow additional funds from the bank for operating the business.

"Let's plow through the rest of the numbers and see where we end up. Accounts receivable, including the $128,000 tax refund, are now $648,000. During the month of April, Zefco will invoice $450,000 in sales and collect, by our calculations, $421,000. Accordingly, accounts receivable at month's end will be $677,000. After deducting the $24,000 of ineligible accounts receivable, the borrowing base on receivables will be $653,000 and, at a margin of 80 percent, availability will be $522,000.

"Inventory should end the month of April at about $585,000. Given lower sales volume and a modest improvement in inventory turnover, this asset category should decrease continually throughout most of the year. At the current 30 percent advance rate, availability of borrowed funds at the end of April should be $175,000.

"Thus," the consultant continued, "the total loan available to Zefco under the accounts receivable and inventory revolving line of credit at the end of April is forecasted to be $687,000.

"Zefco is now borrowing only $650,000 under this credit facility, so the bank should feel reasonably well secured—for the moment. That's the good news. The bad news will begin to surface before you catch your breath.

"Cash disbursements in April are forecasted at $514,000; collections at $421,000—the difference is $93,000. If the bank lends Zefco all of the funds it needs to operate, its revolving loan to the company will increase to $743,000 and that means the

TABLE 4–3

Zefco Container Mfg. Co., Inc.
Cash Flow Forecast—Worst Case Scenario
Cash Disbursements for the Twelve Months Ending March 31, 1986
(in thousands of dollars)

	Apr	May	Jun	Jul	Aug	Sep	Oct	Nov	Dec	Jan	Feb	Mar	Total
Cash disbursements:													
For operations													
Purchases	212	202	195	192	192	192	192	192	192	192	192	192	2337
Wages, salaries, benefits, and payroll taxes	133	131	128	127	127	127	127	127	127	132	132	132	1550
Rent on building	13	13	13	13	12	13	13	13	13	12	13	13	154
Repair and maintenance	12	12	12	14	15	16	16	14	12	12	12	12	159
Telephone and utilities	12	12	11	11	11	11	11	11	11	11	11	11	134
Insurance	6	6	6	6	6	6	6	6	6	6	6	6	72
Truck operating expense	2	1	2	1	2	1	2	1	2	1	2	1	18
Auto operating expense	2	2	2	2	2	2	2	2	2	2	2	2	24
Rent on office equipment	1	1	1	1	1	1	1	1	1	1	1	1	12
Office expenses	3	3	4	3	3	4	3	3	4	3	3	4	40
Professional services	10	10	10	8	8	7	7	9	8	20	8	7	112
Travel and entertainment	2	1	1	1	2	1	1	1	2	1	1	1	15
Taxes and licenses	1	1	1	2	2	1	1	1	3	2	1	3	17
Miscellaneous mfg. expenses	2	2	2	2	2	1	2	2	1	0	2	1	20
Dues and subscriptions	0	0	0	0	0	1	0	0	1	0	0	0	4
Other operating expenses	3	3	3	3	3	3	3	3	3	3	3	3	36
Subtotal	414	400	391	385	387	387	387	386	388	400	389	390	4704

Cash Flow Forecast—Worst Case Scenario
Cash Disbursements for the Twelve Months Ending March 31, 1986
(in thousands of dollars)

	Apr	May	Jun	Jul	Aug	Sep	Oct	Nov	Dec	Jan	Feb	Mar	Total
For servicing debt													
Interest													
Bank	15	15	15	15	15	15	15	15	15	15	15	15	180
Others	7	7	7	7	7	7	7	7	7	7	7	7	84
Principal													
Bank	12	12	12	12	12	12	12	12	12	12	12	12	144
Others	8	9	9	9	9	9	8	9	9	9	9	9	106
Leases													
Manufacturing equipment	9	9	9	9	9	9	9	9	9	9	9	9	108
Vehicles	2	2	2	2	2	2	2	2	2	2	2	2	24
Subtotal	53	54	54	54	54	54	54	54	54	54	54	54	646
For reducing prior payables and accruals	20	20	20	20	20	20	20	20	20	20	20	20	240
For overdraft at bank	27												27
Total cash disbursements	514	474	465	459	461	461	460	460	462	474	463	464	5617

bank will be in an overloaned (undercollateralized) position by $46,000.

"Let's roll the numbers for the next 11 months," the consultant added. During the next hour, the CEO and consultant pounded away at their calculators. Their efforts produced the data arrayed in Table 4–4.

"What's the verdict at the bank going to be?" the CEO asked, although he had already surmised that the prospects looked bleak.

"Well," answered the business consultant, "even though this is a worst case scenario and the numbers will be enhanced by modifying some of our assumptions, in my opinion Zefco will continue to be mired in deficit cash flows unless you make what will appear to many of your associates and employees to be draconian changes.

"The bottom line," explained the consultant, "is if we present a cash flow forecast that even remotely resembles the one we just finished, the bank loan officers will be forced to say something like, 'Why don't you just lock the doors and give us the keys. We'll foreclose and then liquidate or sell the business.' Although it doesn't happen that way very often for a company as large as Zefco, there are plenty of precedents. I told you that you probably wouldn't like the outcome of this last exercise."

How right he was. The CEO sat in a cold sweat and thought to himself, "Almost 30 years of work down the drain. How in the hell did I let this happen?"

Before the CEO could sink into a deeper state of depression, the consultant said, "Look, the numbers we just developed can, make that will, change significantly before we meet with the bank. You've got the power to do it, and tomorrow we'll start developing our 'hit list' on expenses. From this point forward, I think you're going to find the situation improving despite the fact that you'll have to order and/or implement unpleasant actions to save Zefco."

"It's almost nine o'clock," the CEO said, "and I'm physically, mentally and emotionally exhausted. Let's pack it up for tonight, shall we?"

The consultant needed no further encouragement. "Let's wait until nine in the morning to get started again," he said as they headed out the door.

TABLE 4-4

Zefco Container Mfg. Co., Inc.
Cash Flow Forecast—Worst Case Scenario
Flow of Funds for the Twelve Months Ending March 31, 1986
(in thousands of dollars)

	Apr	May	Jun	Jul	Aug	Sep	Oct	Nov	Dec	Jan	Feb	Mar	
Cash or (deficit) beginning of period	(27)	0	0	0	0	0	0	0	0	0	0	0	
Accounts receivable beginning of period	648	677	534	518	507	507	509	513	517	525	529	533	
Net sales	450	430	415	405	405	405	405	405	405	405	405	405	
Collections*	(421)	(573)	(431)	(416)	(405)	(403)	(401)	(401)	(401)	(401)	(401)	(401)	
Accounts receivable end of period	677	534	518	507	507	509	513	517	521	529	533	537	
Less ineligible accounts receivable	(24)	(17)	(11)	(11)	(11)	(6)	(8)	(10)	(11)	(12)	(14)	(16)	
Eligible accounts receivable	653	517	507	496	496	503	505	507	510	517	519	521	
Available from bank at 80%	522	414	406	397	397	402	404	410	412	414	415	417	
Inventory end of period	585	559	535	522	522	514	514	514	510	510	510	506	
Available from bank at 30%	175	168	161	157	157	154	154	154	153	153	153	152	
Total revolving loan available (A/R plus inventory)	697	582	567	554	554	556	558	564	565	567	568	569	
Revolving loan balance beginning of period	650	743	644	678	721	777	835	894	953	1014	1087	1149	
Cash disbursements*	514	474	465	459	461	461	460	460	462	474	463	464	5617
Collections*	(421)	(573)	(431)	(416)	(405)	(403)	(401)	(401)	(401)	(401)	(401)	(401)	5055
Revolving loan balance end of period	743	644	678	721	777	835	894	953	1014	1087	1149	1212	
Availability or (overloan) end of period	(46)	(62)	(111)	(167)	(223)	(279)	(336)	(389)	(449)	(520)	(581)	(643)	
Net cash outflow													562

* See Table 4-2
** See Table 4-3

"We'd better make that 10 o'clock," the CEO said. "I've got to catch up on this stack of urgent phone messages and memos."

The sad realities are that CEOs must also manage much of the day-to-day activities in addition to leading the charge on the turnaround. The big challenge is combining and integrating the two in a manner that permits effectiveness.

As he drove home, the CEO thought to himself, "I wonder what the chances of a turnaround really are—50 percent, 75 percent, 25 percent! Whatever, I'm going to give it my best damn shot. The captain always goes down with his ship—or brings it safely into port."

This night was not going to be restless for the CEO. When he arrived at his home he drank a cold beer, assured his wife that everything was going to be fine (she knew he wasn't telling her everything, of course), and fell into a deep sleep.

The CEO and the consultant resumed their meeting at 10 o'clock the next morning as scheduled. "How are you feeling today?" the business advisor inquired.

"Pretty crummy if you really want to know," the CEO answered. "I just found out that there are already rumors of Zefco's demise flying among employees. It won't be long before our customers and vendors start hearing about how bad things are. You know how these things go."

"I sure do," the consultant said, "it's a classic problem in turnaround situations, and no attempt to stifle the rumors will work. They simply have to expire with the passage of time and performance which proves that the business is still viable and will again prosper. When we're fully prepared, we'll have a general meeting with employees to talk about anything on their minds. You can probably plan on such a meeting a week from today." The CEO made a notation in his notebook.

"We're not going to let the doom-and-gloom mentality of others develop into a self-defeating prophesy for you and Zefco," the business advisor continued. "That's not wishful thinking or bravado. There are many action steps that can be evaluated and implemented between now and the end of April that will radically change attitudes and the direction of Zefco's cash flow. Let's list these things in your notebook. Do you want to take a crack at the possible action steps, or should I just get right into them?"

"You're the expert," the CEO said. "You just talk about them, and I'll write them down. Fire away."

The consultant then said, "The following action steps should be carefully considered and, if practicable, executed without delay:"

- Raise prices on all products by 5 percent, effective May 1st
- Reduce materials purchases to 44 percent of forecasted sales for each month
- Analyze cost/price structure of all product lines
- Eliminate 10 percent of the jobs in the company—both direct labor and office staff
- Have senior managers take 10 percent cut in pay
- Consider using an outside payroll service
- Review health insurance program and ask employees to pay more of the premiums
- Suspend company payments to retirement program
- Develop incentive programs to eliminate waste and duplication
- Establish improved commission program for sales force
- Meet with the landlord and seek to renegotiate rent downward, or at least obtain a temporary reduction in monthly payments until profitability is restored
- Test the idea of subleasing excess space
- Look into hiring an exceptionally capable machinery mechanic to reduce outside repair and maintenance costs
- Have 20 percent of all phones removed and eliminate all speaker phones and automatic dialing equipment
- Set up MCI, Sprint or other comparable long distance telephone system
- Ask current and two new general insurance brokers to review coverage and make bids (Is Zefco overinsured?)
- Collect all company gasoline credit cards being used by employees; retain two for use by truck drivers and salespersons, and cancel the others
- Ask the leasing company to repossess all company cars except those used by the sales force

- Resist using outside professional services unless they are absolutely necessary
- Require strict adherence to company policy with respect to expense reimbursement
- Ask the IRS to accept extended payback of delinquent taxes
- Ask the bank to consider interest only on term loans while a repayment plan is being developed
- Ask other lenders to consider interest only on term loans while repayment plan is being developed
- Ask lessors of manufacturing equipment to accept interest only
- Through the local credit managers affiliate, ask general, unsecured creditors for a 90-day moritorium on previously incurred debt while a reorganization plan is developed and
- Establish the CEO as money czar—personally approving all expenditures over $200 and personally signing all checks.

"That should do for starters," the consultant said. "What do you think?"

"Geez, you really are a hatchet man," the CEO replied.

"I'd rather think of myself as a surgeon of sorts," the business advisor said with a wink and a smile.

"Surgeon?" the CEO laughed aloud, "a sophisticated butcher, maybe, but a surgeon, uh, uh." They both had a good laugh.

"Are you ready to develop a new cash flow forecast?" the consultant asked.

"Let's go have lunch first," came the CEO's reply. "By the way, does your meter run during meals?" The consultant nodded yes. "I thought so. How would you like to pick up the tab?"

"No problem," was the answer. "Where's the nearest McDonald's?"

During lunch, the two men spoke at length about the perceived strengths and weaknesses of Zefco's senior managers. As they were leaving the restaurant the CEO said, "I would appreciate it very much if, after our strategic planning meeting this weekend, you would give me your opinion about my key lieutenants. I think I may need to make some changes in that area, too."

For the remainder of that day, the CEO and the consultant ruminated about the steps required to restore Zefco to profitable operations. They kneaded the financial data many times before they were able to produce the "improvements scenario" of the cash flow forecast which appears in Table 4–5, Table 4–6 and Table 4–7.

"I am confident," the consultant said, "that the bank will find the cash flow forecast—improvements scenario—to be reasonable. It should, at the very least, buy Zefco the time it needs to begin getting its house in order. But let me caution you, in the strongest possible terms, if things don't materialize roughly as presented in the forecast, the bank will unquestionably move swiftly to protect its loan principal.

"Your bank uses one of the most respected law firms in Southern California to represent it in insolvency matters. Trust me, if it gets to the point of a legal skirmish with the bank, we're going to need equally capable legal representation. I've got a number of business acquaintances who are attorneys specializing in this area of the law that I'd recommend to you. I'm hoping that we won't need to call one of them for a knock-down, drag-out fight."

The consultant continued, "You call the bank and let them know we're ready for the meeting on Monday morning—right on schedule. While you're doing that, I'll contact the people at CMA (Credit Managers Association of Southern California) and set up a tentative meeting with the manager of the adjustment bureau (the department for financially troubled borrowers) for next Tuesday afternoon.

"I think we're now ready to have that strategic planning meeting with your senior officers and managers over the weekend. Why don't you spend tomorrow on pressing business matters, and I'll prepare an agenda to facilitate an orderly structure for that meeting."

"Sounds good," the CEO replied. "I'll see you on Saturday morning at eight o'clock."

"Perfect," the consultant said. "You've got my home telephone number if something urgent comes up."

TABLE 4–5

Zefco Container Mfg. Co., Inc.
Cash Flow Forecast—Improvements Scenario
Collections for the Twelve Months Ending March 31, 1986
(in thousands of dollars)

	Apr	May	Jun	Jul	Aug	Sep	Oct	Nov	Dec	Jan	Feb	Mar	Total
Net sales estimates	450	451	436	425	425	425	425	425	425	425	425	425	5162
Collection of existing accounts receivable													
Prior to January		7	4	2									13
From January sales	29	13											42
From February sales	55	29	13										97
From March sales	261	57	30	13									361
Subtotal	345	106	47	15									513
Collection of future accounts receivable													
April sales	76	267	58	31	13								445
May sales		77	267	58	31	13							446
June sales			73	259	56	31	13						432
July sales				72	252	55	30	12					421
August sales					72	252	55	30	12				421
September sales						72	252	55	30	12			421
October sales							72	252	55	30	12		421
November sales								72	252	55	30	12	421
December sales									72	252	55	30	409
January sales										72	252	55	379
February sales											72	252	324
March sales												72	72
Subtotal	76	344	398	420	424	423	422	421	421	421	421	421	4612
Collection of tax refund		128											128
Total collections	421	578	445	435	424	423	422	421	421	421	421	421	5253

TABLE 4-6

Zefco Container Mfg, Co., Inc.
Cash Flow Forecast—Improvements Scenario
Cash Disbursements for the Twelve Months Ending March 31, 1986
(in thousands of dollars)

	Apr	May	Jun	Jul	Aug	Sep	Oct	Nov	Dec	Jan	Feb	Mar	Total
Cash disbursements:													
For operations													
Purchases	212	198	192	187	187	187	187	187	187	187	187	187	2285
Wages, salaries, benefits, and payroll taxes	133	118	115	114	113	112	110	110	110	110	110	110	1365
Rent on building	13	13	13	13	12	13	13	13	13	12	13	13	154
Repair and maintenance	12	11	10	11	12	12	12	11	11	11	11	11	135
Telephone and utilities	12	11	10	11	10	11	10	11	10	11	10	11	128
Insurance	6	6	5	6	5	6	5	6	5	6	5	6	67
Truck operating expense	2	1	1	2	1	1	2	1	1	2	1	1	16
Auto operating expense	1	1	1	1	1	1	1	1	1	1	1	1	12
Rent on office equipment	1	1	0	1	1	0	1	1	0	1	1	0	8
Office expenses	3	3	2	3	3	2	3	3	2	3	3	2	33
Professional services	10	10	10	8	8	5	4	2	2	22	2	2	85
Travel and entertainment	2	1	1	1	1	1	1	1	1	1	1	1	13
Taxes and licenses	1	1	1	2	2	1	1	1	1	2	1	3	17
Miscellaneous mfg. expenses	2	2	2	2	2	1	2	2	3	2	2	1	20
Dues and subscriptions	0	0	1	0	0	1	0	0	1	0	0	1	4
Other operating expenses	3	3	2	3	3	2	3	3	2	3	3	2	32
Subtotal	413	380	366	363	360	357	355	352	351	374	351	352	4374

TABLE 4–6 (*Continued*)

Zefco Container Mfg. Co., Inc.
Cash Flow Forecast—Improvements Scenario
Cash Disbursements for the Twelve Months Ending March 31, 1986
(in thousands of dollars)

	Apr	May	Jun	Jul	Aug	Sep	Oct	Nov	Dec	Jan	Feb	Mar	Total
For servicing debt													
Interest													
Bank	15	15	15	15	15	15	15	15	15	15	15	15	180
Others	7	7	7	7	7	7	7	7	7	7	7	7	84
Principal													
Bank	12	12	12	12	12	12	12	12	12	12	12	12	144
Others	8	0	0	0	9	9	9	9	9	8	9	9	79
Leases													
Manufacturing equipment	9	9	9	9	9	9	9	9	9	9	9	9	108
Vehicles	2	1	0	1	0	1	0	1	0	1	0	1	8
Subtotal	53	44	43	44	52	53	52	53	52	52	52	53	603
For reducing prior payables and accruals	0	0	0	0	10	10	10	12	12	12	15	15	96
For overdraft at bank	27												27
Total cash disbursements	493	424	409	407	422	420	417	417	415	438	418	420	5100

TABLE 4–7

Zefco Container Mfg. Co., Inc.
Cash Flow Forecast—Improvements Scenario
Flow of Funds for the Twelve Months Ending March 31, 1986
(in thousands of dollars)

	Apr	May	Jun	Jul	Aug	Sep	Oct	Nov	Dec	Jan	Feb	Mar	
Cash or (deficit) beginning of period	(27)	0	0	0	0	0	0	0	0	0	0	0	
Accounts receivable beginning of period	648	677	550	541	531	532	534	537	541	545	549	553	
Net sales	450	451	436	425	425	425	425	425	425	425	425	425	5100
Collections*	(421)	(578)	(445)	(435)	(424)	(423)	(422)	(421)	(421)	(421)	(421)	(421)	5253
Accounts receivable end of period	677	550	541	531	532	534	537	541	545	549	553	557	
Less ineligible accounts receivable	(24)	(17)	(16)	(16)	(16)	(16)	(16)	(16)	(16)	(17)	(17)	(17)	
Eligible accounts receivable	653	533	525	515	516	518	521	525	529	532	536	540	
Available from bank at 80%	522	426	420	412	413	414	417	420	423	426	429	432	
Inventory end of period	585	575	560	550	540	530	520	515	510	510	505	505	
Available from bank at 30%	175	173	168	165	162	159	156	155	153	153	152	152	
Total revolving loan available (A/R plus inventory)	697	599	588	577	575	573	573	575	576	579	581	584	
Revolving loan balance beginning of period	650	722	568	532	504	502	499	494	490	484	501	498	
Cash disbursements**	493	424	409	407	422	420	417	417	415	438	418	420	
Collections*	(421)	(578)	(445)	(435)	(424)	(423)	(422)	(421)	(421)	(421)	(421)	(421)	
Revolving loan balance end of period	722	568	532	504	502	499	494	490	484	501	498	497	
Availability or (overloan) end of period	(25)	31	56	73	73	74	79	85	92	78	83	87	
Net cash inflow													153

* See Table 4–5
** See Table 4–6

Chapter

5

Developing a New Strategic Plan for Zefco

The consultant knew from his experience in organizing and leading numerous strategic planning sessions that it would be vitally important to have a well-structured outline from which he and Zefco's CEO could work. Well-planned meetings are always desirable, but they are especially necessary for financially troubled businesses. Participants tend to be less cooperative and open than they are when they are employed by a smooth running, profitable company.

The predominant fear of everyone is that they will be held personally accountable for the problems. Everyone presumes that the boss has a hidden agenda and is looking for scapegoats, and no one wishes to be subjected to the adverse consequences that would logically follow if they were identified as the culprits. No one wished to be terminated—fired.

With the above situation in mind, the business advisor prepared the outline which follows:

1. The hard facts and figures shown in the worst case scenario of the cash flow forecast will be reviewed.

   a. Zefco is continuing to lose money at a disastrous rate.

    b. Changes must be made swiftly or all creditor support will vanish.

2. A reassessment of Zefco's mission is essential.

    a. The new objectives must reflect the company's precarious financial condition and be oriented to survival.

    b. Zefco's core business purpose.

    c. The question that must be answered is "What can Zefco do without?"—not "What can Zefco do?"

    d. Zefco must become a dictatorship for awhile.

    e. The required paradigm shift is not everyone's cup of tea.

3. An environmental scan must be made.

    a. Zefco can't change the direction of the economy.

    b. A review of the economy is needed:

        1. Federal budget deficits;
        2. Monetary policy of the Federal Reserve Bank;
        3. Real interest rates and accessibility to capital;
        4. Continued growth or a recession?
        5. Implications for Zefco.

    c. Have Zefco's customers expressed any concern about the company's ability to provide products of good quality, serviceability and reliability?

    d. Are Zefco's employees aware of the facts?

        1. Do they feel they've been kept in the dark?
        2. Is there an information void developing?

            a. If so, it will be filled by inaccurate or incomplete data if not addressed quickly and discussed openly.
            b. It will lead to a demoralized workforce.

    e. Zefco's competitors will try to capitalize on the company's unfortunate situation with:

        1. Predatory pricing tactics;
        2. Rumor-mongering regarding Zefco's imminent collapse;
        3. Pirating of key production workers or staff.

4. The hard facts and figures shown in the "improvements scenario" of the cash flow forecast:

   a. Raise prices, not unit volume;
   b. Identify product lines that are not profitable;
   c. Cut operating expenses wherever possible;
   d. Provide leadership by example:

      1. Salary reduction and longer workweek;
      2. Perquisites elimination.

5. Translation of Zefco's new strategic plan into financial terms that can be presented to all stakeholders in the company.

   a. Pro forma statements of operations.
   b. Pro forma balance sheets.

6. Presentation of a comprehensive list of steps taken recently and those to be taken in the future.

When he finished writing the outline, the consultant called Zefco's CEO and said, "I know we hadn't planned on this, but I think it might be useful to both of us if we get together before tomorrow's strategic planning meeting to go over the agenda I've prepared. Are you available late this afternoon or early evening?"

"Well," the CEO answered, "Friday evenings are generally reserved for dinner out with the family, but if you think it's really necessary I'll cancel."

"I think a meeting beforehand is needed," the business advisor explained, "but we could have it early tomorrow morning if you'd prefer."

"How early and where?" the CEO asked.

"Six thirty at the coffee shop down the street from your office," said the consultant.

"Okay, that would be better for me. I'll see you there," the CEO said.

The next morning the CEO and the consultant met as arranged. Shortly after they were seated in the restaurant, the business advisor handed a copy of the agenda to the CEO. After perusing the document, the CEO said, "This looks fine to me. It's a good synopsis of what we've been talking about for the past few days, and I think my associates will find little to quarrel about in it. Particularly, since last weekend we had a long discussion among ourselves and they've been somewhat conditioned to expect the hard times you've described."

"Excellent," said the consultant, who was given to using superlatives, "I was hoping you'd be agreeable. I think we should now discuss our respective roles in the strategic planning meeting. I'm prepared to accept as much or as little responsibility as you wish me to have. I could, for example, act as chairman or secretary for the entire planning session while your associates *and* you primarily respond to the material in the outline. I strongly suggest, however, that you *not* let me lead the meeting. It will most assuredly convey to your subordinates that Zefco is in the process of becoming other-directed rather than inner-directed. I also—"

"Hey," the CEO interrupted, "I *intend* to chair this meeting. I fully appreciate the risks involved in not keeping a firm hold on the reins. I won't allow myself to be relegated to the position of de facto subordinate. Either I run this company, or I leave. I know I need your help in learning the ropes of this turnaround business, but I am going to stay in control of the process."

"Your attitude is terrific!" the consultant said. "I can see right now that this is going to be a very productive meeting. How do you intend to explain my presence and participation in the meeting?"

"I won't have any problem with that," the CEO said. "Just leave it up to me. Let's buy a dozen donuts for the troops and head on over to the plant."

The CEO and the consultant arrived at Zefco shortly before eight o'clock. Uncharacteristically, all of the key managers were there early. They obviously recognized the importance of the meeting and clearly did not want to show up after it had started. After a few uneasy moments of small talk, the meeting began.

"Folks," the CEO began, "I know I've been pretty much inaccessible to you for the past few days, and I apologize. As this meeting unfolds, though, I think you'll see why I've had my door closed. First, I should introduce this gentleman, and I use that term loosely. (The group of managers smiled a bit.) He's a business advisor specializing in assisting financially troubled companies like ours. According to people I've spoken to, he has developed a reputation for helping businesses avoid the necessity—and the expense—of using the bankruptcy court to get the time needed to achieve a turnaround.

"Quite honestly," he continued, "I wish to hell we didn't need his services. But the immutable fact is that survival planning requires fast and fluid, yet flexible responses. None of us is experienced in these matters. He has been very helpful to me already in gaining a good overview of the turnaround process. He also has had a great deal of experience in negotiating with general creditors and bankers in situations like Zefco's.

"Let's face it, our credibility as managers is at a low ebb. You know how queasy our bankers feel. We cannot afford to make any additional errors in judgment. I wanted someone who could coach us through our troubles. And he's the person I've chosen.

"How's that for an introduction?" the CEO said as he looked at the consultant.

"I don't think I could have said it any better," the consultant answered.

The CEO seemed confident as he readied himself for the presentation of the unpleasant business at hand.

"Shall we start?" he asked.

There was no immediate reply. After a few seconds, he continued, "Let's take a look at some of the hard realities confronting our company."

With that, he passed around copies of the worst case scenario of the cash flow forecast. For the next five minutes or so, everyone intently studied the information before them.

"Well, team," the CEO said matter-of-factly, "Zefco is losing money for the simplest of reasons—we're spending one hell of a lot more than we're receiving. I think we all know as a result of last week's meeting the causes of Zefco's troubles. I don't want to rehash any of those discussions. The situation is no longer tolerable or acceptable. In the consultant's opinion *and* mine, Zefco will lose the complete support and cooperation of its creditors without significant changes. If that happens, we'd better duck for cover."

Silence again prevailed in the meeting room. Even the

consultant was taken aback by the CEO's forcefulness. The business advisor was in wholehearted agreement with the CEO's approach, but he didn't really anticipate the speed with which the CEO had apparently grasped the severity of the problems. It typically requires a minimum of a few weeks of being buffeted from all sides before an incumbent CEO comes to grips with the realities of the steps needed to start a turnaround. The consultant was impressed, and he made a note to himself to relate his surprise and pleasure with the CEO's command of the situation.

Judging from the facial expressions of the other Zefco managers, they too, were mildly shocked by the CEO's change in demeanor in making his remarks. Such a display was apparently unusual for him. The consultant was pleased by this as well because the changes in corporate culture at Zefco would need to be embraced by all of the CEO's lieutenants if the turnaround effort were to be successful.

"We've got to completely reassess Zefco's mission," the CEO continued. "What is the purpose, the mission, of this company?" the CEO said looking directly at his vice president of marketing.

The marketing manager, unable to dodge the question, took a deep breath and replied glibly, "We're in the business of manufacturing a line of specialty metal, composite and plastic containers. At least, I think we're in that business."

"Good try, but wrong," the CEO replied. Then staring at the personnel manager he said, "What's your opinion?"

"I'd say," the personnel manager answered, "that Zefco's basic mission is to satisfy its customers' needs in their efforts to sell their products to consumers in attractive containers. Without our customers, we'd be out of business."

Once again the CEO said, "Good try, but you're also off the mark."

Without prompting, the accounting manager offered, "Won't this be a moot point if we don't convince the bank and the creditors that Zefco is a viable company?"

"Perfect!" the CEO said excitedly. "Zefco's primary mission at this moment in history is to survive! The company's financial condition is so tenuous and precarious that we must do everything we can to demonstrate to our stakeholders (employees, bankers, creditors, the IRS, etc.) that a turnaround is underway.

Zefco's core business purpose is now to earn a profit. We must concern ourselves with doing more while having less. This strategic planning meeting is not focusing on what Zefco can do. We want to determine what this company can do *without*.

"The atmosphere around Zefco is likely to be, in fact will be, quite a bit different from what you are accustomed to. You know that in the past my style of management has been to delegate significant amounts of authority and then to stay out of the way of individual managers. In fact, some of you have criticized me for being somewhat cavalier. Well, as of right now, Zefco will be run as an autocracy with myself as the dictator as well as the chief cook and bottle washer. My entire net worth is at risk, and I've got to do what is necessary to preserve some if not all of it.

"I accept full responsibility for any mistakes that have been made in the past or will be made in the future," the CEO continued. "Look, I'm not out to get anyone. I'm going to need one heck of a lot of help to do this job right. That's why I've retained a turnaround specialist and why I've asked you to meet with me today. Following orders is not for everyone, I realize. If some of you are unprepared or unwilling to accept the new regimen, I will understand if you decide to leave the company. Would anyone care to comment?"

"Holy [expletive deleted]!" the marketing vice president said (and other managers probably thought). "Don't you think you're going a little overboard with the iron hand approach. That's a 180 degree turn, and it seems like a knee-jerk reaction to me. It also sounds like someone else is putting words in your mouth." He then nervously looked around the room for signs of support. There was none to be found.

"Uh oh," the marketing manager thought to himself, "it looks like I've put my big foot in my mouth again."

He felt even worse when the vice president of engineering said "I'm 110 percent in favor of the CEO's decision. I support it all the way." A few of the others appeared to nod their approval of that comment.

Everyone, including the CEO was quite uneasy about what might be said next. Sensing that an ice-breaker was necessary, the consultant said, "I'm sure some of you folks think that your boss and I planned and rehearsed this scene previously, but quite honestly, we did not. He and I have obviously spoken a great deal about what I think is ahead for Zefco, but your CEO has made the independent judgment about how *he* should proceed. I'm in complete agreement with his approach because I have seen it work over and over again.

"Any efforts to maintain the status quo will be futile. In fact, they will be met with increasing levels of hostility aimed at your boss—from people and organizations that have the clout to force substantive changes directly on Zefco and indirectly on you. Even if you don't want to accept these statements as dogma, you should give the CEO a chance. The alternative is probably failure of the business."

Glancing at his outline, the CEO said, "I think we should move along to the next topic."

The vice president of marketing, breathing a sigh of relief thought to himself, "I'm not positive but I think I just dodged a bullet. For crying out loud, why can't I shut up?"

"Okay," the CEO continued, "we need to take a hard look at the environment which affects Zefco. I'd sincerely like all of you to make inputs on Zefco's external threats and opportunities as well as its internal weaknesses and strengths.

"Our company can't change the direction of the economy nor can we ignore it. Let's talk economics. Our friendly consultant here is a student of the dismal science. What does your crystal ball say about the economy for the next year or two?"

"I have some very definite views on the subject that I'd be happy to share with you," the consultant answered. "First, the federal budget deficit is and will probably remain appallingly high for several more years. There are a great many political action groups and special interest groups wielding so much power that I personnally find it hard to imagine that the administration and the congress will institute the measures needed to attack the budgetary problems in a meaningful way. However, the situation cannot continue on ad infinitum. The mechanism used to cure fiscal and financial irresponsibility in our economic system is called a depression. And I think a 1930s-type economic contraction is quite conceivable. It darn near happened four years ago.

"Second," he continued, "the monetary policy of the Federal

Reserve Bank will very likely remain relatively tight for the indefinite future. The deficits must be financed in some manner and the Fed is the agency used to accommodate the sale of securities by the U.S. Treasury and other government agencies.

"One of the Fed's avowed goals is to keep inflation under control. In order to achieve that objective, it has chosen to keep the growth in the money supply within a specified range. The growth targets in place suggest a continuation of a tighter credit policy. As always with the Fed, however, there will be abrupt starts and stops.

"Third," the consultant continued, "the seemingly conflicting objectives of fiscal and monetary policy makers suggest, to me at least, that interest rates will remain high. There probably won't be any crowding out of borrowers. Any individual, business or institution willing and able to pay high real rates of interest will likely have funds made available.

"Lenders, on the whole, have done a good job over the past five to 10 years in figuring out how to shift the interest rate risk from themselves to their borrowers. Most of the funds lent out nowadays are on short term, floating rate bases. Unfortunately, they've done a rather poor job in evaluating the creditworthiness of their borrowers—witness the international debt situation and the number of U.S. business failures that have occurred during the past half dozen years. In my opinion, we have entered a period of high real financing costs—businesses should be trying to find ways to definance not refinance.

"And fourth," the consultant concluded, "I think all of the above adds up to a recession, or worse, in the not too distant future. If an economic downturn is looming on the horizon, the implication for Zefco is that decisions must be made even more quickly then would otherwise be necessary."

"I wish I could disagree with that scenario," the CEO said, "but everything I read seems to suggest the same economic outlook. Highly leveraged small and medium-sized businesses like Zefco are in a real bind. Price increases will be extremely hard to implement and hold if a recession develops, and borrowing costs will continue to be onerous. I guess our original 1985 sales forecast for Zefco was more bullish than circumstances probably warranted.

"So much for the big picture," the CEO continued. "Let's discuss some of Zefco's closer-to-home issues. We all know how important our customers are. Have there been *any* complaints from customers about product quality?" he asked the vice president of production.

"No, sirree," came the production manager's reply. "We haven't had any products returned for nearly a year. In fact, from what I hear through the grapevine, Zefco is producing about the best quality products in town."

"To what do you attribute that record?" the CEO asked.

"Well, two things come to mind," the production vice president answered. "Number one, we hired a QC (quality control) man to make sure that nothing left the plant that wasn't up to snuff. And number two, we (actually the vice president of engineering) made some enhancements to the product specifications to ensure that our quality improved."

The consultant made a note to find out if perhaps the QC person was doing too good a job. For example, how many products are rejected internally and discarded? The affect on cost of sales could be substantial.

"If Zefco is producing containers of superior quality why isn't it getting premium prices?" the CEO asked, turning to the vice president of marketing.

"Are you sure you want me to answer that question?" said the now reticent marketing manager.

"[Expletive deleted!]" snapped the CEO, "if you're not going to be part of the solution, you're part of the problem. If it's the latter, you might as well get the hell out of here and let us get on with our business."

After a few taut seconds which seemed like hours, the vice president of marketing said, "I apologize to all of you. I just didn't want to be the bearer of any more bad tidings. The truth is, the marketplace does not require products of Zefco's high quality. Mind you, our customers love our products and, all other things being equal, they'll take a Zefco container over most any other. But if we're not in line on pricing we'll lose the business. Zefco has overcompensated for past mistakes in quality control."

"That message has powerful implications," the consultant

remarked. "By extension, if the requirement for quality control and product quality per se are lessening, Zefco should be able to at least maintain prices while reducing costs to a significant degree. Less raw material would be needed; fewer man-hours could be spent on QC; and perhaps fewer products would be thrown away as scrap. I would say that customer relationships at this point are the least of Zefco's worries.

"The low average collection period of accounts receivable is another indication that Zefco enjoys a good overall relationship with its customers. Satisfied customers pay their bills—assuming they are good payers to start with. We're going to want to keep up the excellent rapport with Zefco's customers and assure them of continued good quality, serviceability and reliability, but at least we won't need to spend a great deal of time shoring up a weak part of the company's business—as is the case in many turnaround situations."

"Well, there's some sunshine after all," the CEO said cheerfully. "Maybe we've done something too well. If we just gravitate to slightly above the median in product quality we should still be in decent shape with our source of revenues. It will take marketing savvy to accomplish the objective, but I think we can do it.

"How are the other employees taking all of this?" the CEO inquired.

The personnel manager, who is well piped into Zefco's informal communication system, said, "For the most part people are really unsure about what is going on. There is great apprehension that the company could be forced to shut its doors. They are obviously very concerned that everyone could soon be collecting unemployment checks instead of paychecks."

The production manager added, "We've got a very solid and supportive group of nonunion workers out there in the plant. Believe it or not, they've asked me what *they* can do to help Zefco pull through. Their biggest concern is that they don't know what's happening, and they're afraid that if the worst happens it will come unannounced, and they won't be prepared."

"It's amazing," the CEO said, "how fast news travels. Three weeks ago we were all sitting around fat, dumb and happy, and now the whole world seems to know how dirty our laundry is."

The CEO continued, "Next week we're going to have a meeting with all employees to discuss this situation openly. I'll spend the entire day if necessary answering every question."

The consultant added, "Nearly every financially troubled business with which I have worked has developed at least a temporary and occasionally a permanent information void. I feel certain in telling you that in the absence of factual presentations by management, the void will quite probably be filled by inaccurate or incomplete data. And that could lead to a dissipirited, demoralized workforce.

"One other thing," the consultant continued, "your friendly competitors will try, if they haven't already begun, to take advantage of Zefco's problems by: going after the company's customers with predatory pricing tactics; spreading rumors about the company being on the verge of bankruptcy; and attempting to steal some of your best employees. If that seems callous and unsporting to you, remember this: one company's problems are another company's opportunities. There are many competitors who will be looking to apply the knockout punch to Zefco."

"His message is 'keep your ears to the ground,'" the CEO said. "I want to know if anything like that happens. If it does, I will call the CEO of the offending company and tell him or her where we stand. We're going to protect our turf, no doubt about it."

Up to this point most of the discussion had a decidedly philosophical bent—no real substance as regards individual financial sacrifices. The next part of the strategic planning meeting would have a definite dollars and cents overtone. The CEO suggested that a coffee break might be a good idea. As the other managers headed for the coffee pot, he asked the consultant, "How'm I doin'?"

"Fantastically," the consultant whispered, "and I mean that sincerely."

"I know I shouldn't be feeling good about these proceedings," the CEO said, "but there seems to be a certain missionary zeal in me for the first time in quite a few years. I'm actually beginning to believe that a turnaround is in the cards for Zefco."

After the brief respite, the CEO resumed the meeting by handing out copies of the improvements scenario of the cash flow forecast.

"Brace yourselves," the CEO said to his associates, "now comes the real gist of our meeting. Let's first compare the net cash flow figures of the two forecasts. If the company were to continue the way it is going—the worst case scenario—Zefco would incur about $562,000 in negative cash flow over the next 12 months [see bottom line, Table 4–4]. We know that scenario won't fly. Now, as shown in the improvements scenario, by making a number of difficult but essential changes we can produce a positive cash flow of approximately $153,000 over the same period [see bottom line, Table 4–7]. That is a swing of $715,000!

"I suspect we have a few doubting Thomases in the room," the CEO continued, "but at the conclusion of this planning session you should all be believers. Again, no one will be forced to accept the new strategic plan—although Zefco has become a dictatorship, involuntary servitude is not part of the program."

This gallows humor was greeted with the faintest of grins.

"I must insist, however, that once we decide on the specifics of the turnaround plan, everyone pulls together.

"Okay, here's what we've got to do. First, we're going to raise prices—5 percent is what I've got in mind. I know we're going to suffer some drop in volume, and the marketing department is going to be working its tail off keeping the orders flowing, but we've got to do it. Who knows, maybe our competitors will follow our lead and raise their prices to match ours.

"Second," the CEO continued, "we've got to identify product lines that do not currently contribute to profitability; then we've either got to make them into winners or eliminate them. This process won't happen overnight, but, believe me, we're going over this area with a fine-tooth comb.

"Would you like to add anything to my last statement?" the CEO said to the consultant.

"Yes, thanks," the business advisor answered. "To the extent that Zefco is successful in achieving a gross profit (or a higher gross profit) on all of its various products, it will mean less austere measures are needed in reducing other operating expenses."

The CEO continued his list with, "Third, we've got to cut expenses drastically. If you compare the forecasts, you'll see that the total dollar amount of required reductions in cash disbursements for operations between the two scenarios is $330,000 [refer to Tables 4–3 and 4–6]. Although we have identified cuts in nearly every category of expenditure, two types of expenses stand out prominently—purchases and payroll.

"I am somewhat heartened to have heard earlier that the overall quality of Zefco's products is so outstanding. That tells me we can achieve, if not exceed, the planned reduction in purchases when we marginally decrease the product specifications to industry norms.

"Now the toughest part," the CEO continued. "We must reduce our payroll costs. Through some combination of a reduced head count and lower pay and benefits we've got to cut expenses in this area by nearly 12 percent. On Monday morning we are going to dismiss five people (about 10 percent of total employment). I'm going to leave it up to you to decide the names of the individuals who get laid off, but I want to deliver the bad news to each of them personally.

"There's more, unfortunately. We've got to demonstrate to our remaining employees (in addition to various groups of the creditors) that we, too, are going to suffer. We must lead by example. Accordingly, effective immediately I am reducing my salary by 10 percent and your salaries by 5 percent. In addition, most of the perquisites that we've all come to enjoy will be eliminated."

"Does that include automobiles and fees at the club?" asked the vice president of engineering who is an avid golfer.

"Regrettably, yes," came the CEO's reply. "We've got about 30 days before the leasing company repossesses the cars. You have two options really: buy yourself a new car, or take over the lease payments on your present company car. Also, Zefco won't be paying for vehicle operating expenses anymore unless proper documentation for business usage accompanies your expense reimbursement requests.

"I'm acutely, painfully, aware that I am asking you to make substantial financial sacrifices along with me. We've all enjoyed the good life at Zefco for a number of years. It's time for the company and for us to live the Spartan life for a while. I'm too old to start looking for another job or career, but some of you might well want to consider that alternative now that you know what's in store. If any of you opt to leave Zefco, I want you to know that I'll be happy to give you a strong recommendation if needed. Any questions?"

"It sounds a little like your looking for volunteers to quit," the personnel manager said only half-jokingly.

The CEO replied, "I hope that I haven't conveyed that message. That's not at all what I'm trying to communicate. I'm just attempting to level with everyone. I don't want to find out in a month or two that someone didn't fully understand what's really happening around Zefco."

"How long will it be necessary for us to remain at the lower salaries and benefits?" asked the accounting manager who has three young children.

"I don't know the answer to that," the CEO said. "Would you like to try and field the question?" he asked the consultant.

"I'll give you an educated guess. First off, though, as long as you remain in management control of the company, you can pay yourself whatever you like. Creditors at this point have no say in Zefco's internal affairs. I can tell you this much—they'll applaud what's about to be done.

"To answer the question more directly," the consultant continued, "it will probably be a year or more before Zefco can reinstate any of the cutbacks discussed today."

There was a long silence and a pall seemed to envelop the room. It finally hit home with all of Zefco's managers that a turnaround would materially upset their heretofore relatively stable company—and their own wallets.

"I know exactly how you feel," the CEO said. "Two days ago I felt like I'd been run over by a speeding truck. I brooded most of yesterday, but I overcame that blue funk and you will, too. I know you'd all like to adjourn to Clancy's [the local bar and grill] and drown a few sorrows, but I want you to bear down one more time today and come up with the names of the people we need to let go. Then we'll have a beer or two. While you're doing your nasty deed, the consultant and I will be working on some of the other objectives we need to specify."

The consultant and the CEO left the others in the conference room to go to the CEO's office.

"I feel nauseous," the CEO said as he sat down. "That's one of the more distasteful and difficult things I've ever had to do. I'm not sure I'm really cut out for the part of the villian in a black hat. My emotions keep racing up and down. It's nerve wracking."

"Fine," the consultant said. "Does that mean you're ready to throw in the towel and walk away from the problems?"

"You. . . . You're merciless," the CEO replied. "Can't I wallow around in even a little self-pity and remorse?"

"Maybe later this afternoon at Clancy's, but right now we've got other things to discuss. In the past week you have exhibited phenomenal ability to absorb information about how to survive a financial trauma. Most of what you've learned thus far has dealt with the internal dynamics of a turnaround. To be sure, there are numerous other Zefco-related tasks to assign or to do yourself. For the moment, though, I'd like to concentrate on how Zefco can best communicate with its external publics."

"Its what?" the CEO asked.

"Primarily, Zefco's bankers and trade creditors," the business advisor answered. "There are probably going to be 10 to 20 separate and/or joint meetings with those groups over the next several months. Although they generally will listen with some interest to all of the wonderful things Zefco is doing, they will be concerned primarily with one thing—when do they get their money back?

"To get and retain their cooperation," the consultant continued, "Zefco's new strategic plan must contain long-term objectives that are measurable and achievable. They will be looking for ways to keep Zefco's feet to the fire. The cash flow forecast is a good, but not a sufficient, start for a turnaround program."

"What else do we need, then?" the CEO asked.

"Before we meet with the general creditors in about two weeks, we must translate Zefco's new strategic plan into concise financial terms. More specifically, we'll need pro forma statements of operations and balance sheets with accompanying assumptions for the next three years.

"Finally, we should present a comprehensive list of the steps that will have been taken by our meeting date and those that will be completed in the future."

"And who is going to prepare those pro forma financial

statements?" the CEO asked. "Never mind, you don't need to answer—it's us, isn't it?" The consultant nodded. "Okay," the CEO said, "let's go back and finish our meeting with the troops."

As the CEO and the consultant entered the conference room, the personnel manager said, "We seem to have reached an impasse. We've identified four people but everyone else appears to be indispensible."

"Let me see the list of names, please," the CEO said. "These people are all production workers. This is not acceptable." Looking at the vice president of production, the CEO said, "Can you really make do with that big a cut in labor?"

"It will be an extremely tight squeeze, but we'll somehow do it," was the reply.

The CEO said, "I want to know immediately if you have any problems with getting products out the door. If so, you have my permission to hire back one of the workers. Well, I guess I'll have to break the log jam. Your administrative assistant," the CEO said looking at the personnel manager, "and one of your two salespeople," he said motioning to the marketing manager, "will have to be let go."

"I can't do my job effectively without some help," the vice president of personnel implored.

"You and I will share my secretary's time," the CEO answered.

The marketing manager was seething but bit his lip and said nothing.

"Oh, I just remembered I have a meeting with the bank at nine o'clock Monday morning," the CEO said. "I'll meet with the affected employees in the afternoon instead of the time originally planned. Now, would anyone like to join me at Clancy's to commiserate?"

There was no sign of interest. The CEO was a tad disappointed but not really surprised that none of his managers wanted to join him. He made no effort to coax them. It was apparent that his subordinates just wanted to get out of there.

"Okay," he said, "the meeting is adjourned. I'll see you all on Monday."

With those words, the Zefco managers departed, most with their eyes diverted from the CEO's. The CEO and the consultant went to the tavern to review the meeting and soothe their spirits.

"How do you think they'll respond?" the CEO asked.

"It could take a few days, but I think most of them will accept the reality of what Zefco must do, and they'll rally to support you."

"What were your impressions about my vice president of marketing? I darn near fired him back there."

"I'd rather reserve judgment about any of your subordinates until I've had a chance to work more closely with them in the next few weeks."

After another round, they finished their meeting and headed home for the remainder of a short weekend.

Chapter

6

Negotiating with Various Creditor Groups

At eight o'clock on the following Monday morning, the CEO and the consultant met again to plan their encounter with Zefco's bankers.

"What do we need to take with us to the meeting?" the CEO asked.

"Two things", the consultant answered. "The improvements scenario of the cash flow forecast; and the documentation relating to the tax refund claim."

The CEO called his accounting manager and requested that the latter data be sent over right away.

"What do we want to accomplish at today's meeting?" the CEO inquired further.

"We have seven specific objectives on our agenda," the consultant responded. "First, we want to convince your bankers that Zefco is indeed viable. Second, we want to persuade those officials that the company should not require new loans from the bank or other external sources. Third, we want to explain, step-by-step if necessary, how the revolving loan balance will decrease from the $700,000 range and stabilize at about $500,000.

"Fourth, we want to show that a safety factor has been built into the cash flow forecast—that is, Zefco plans to borrow less than would normally be available to it under the formula. This will ensure that the bank's revolving loan remains well collateralized. Fifth, we want to emphasize that the principal payments on the bank's term loan will be made as previously agreed, and that interest payments will be kept current."

"Sixth," the consultant continued, "we want to assure the bank that none of its future loan advances under the revolving line of credit will be used to repay previously incurred debt. In other words, Zefco will seek a temporary, noncourt-ordered moratorium on its debts to unsecured creditors. We'll be talking a lot more about this after the bankers' meeting. And seventh, we want the credit people at the bank to know that Zefco will take the necessary steps to assure the bank that its security interests will remain senior to those of the Internal Revenue Service and the California Franchise Tax Board."

The CEO said, "I don't quite understand the last point. How could the bank's security position be threatened by the taxing authorities? Doesn't the bank have a clear, priority position?

The consultant said, "Let me expand on that subject a bit. The problem concerns not current but future debt. If we are unsuccessful in arranging a subordination agreement and/or a stretched-out plan of repayment for delinquent payroll taxes, the IRS and the state could file liens against Zefco's assets. If that occurs, the company has 45 days to clean up the back payroll taxes. Failing that, the tax claims become senior to *new* credit extended to Zefco.

"The bank is unlikely to allow that to happen. In practice, the bank would threaten to stop funding Zefco. The IRS and the state don't want to be responsible for putting companies out of business if there is a decent chance that the business will recover so they usually cooperate with reasonable requests. Nevertheless, it's something we must be sure doesn't fall through the cracks."

"Let's hit the road," the CEO said as he started walking to the door. "I'd like to get to the bank a little early if we can. You know I haven't felt this prepared for a test since I sat for a bacteriology exam when I was a junior in college. And I aced that one!"

As they drove together to the bank's regional headquarters in downtown Los Angeles, the advisor said, "I think we've got an excellent chance of selling our program to the bank officials. Don't misunderstand me, they're probably going to continue with the hard line approach, but I think this cash flow forecast will give them something to latch on to—for the time being at least."

"Let's hope so," the CEO said. "I still don't want to pursue the alternatives."

When the CEO and the consultant arrived, they were taken to the bank's well-appointed conference room and offered coffee. After a few minutes, the loan officer and the senior credit administrator arrived, accompanied by two of the bank's outside attorneys—one of whom the consultant knew to be a specialist in bankruptcy law. That did not bode well.

The consultant's opening remark was, "I'm a little surprised, guys. We weren't really expecting the bank to bring its legal counsel into this meeting. We thought it was going to be a discussion of business-related issues."

"The lawyers are here on a stand-by basis, that's all," said the bank credit officer. "It's part of the bank's newly instituted contingency planning for potential problem loans."

"Oh, I wasn't aware of the new policy," the consultant said, but he was thinking, "I doubt that answer—the bank must believe Zefco's problems are pretty bad." Whatever the real motivation for the attorneys' presence, the consultant felt that Zefco's CEO was ready to give a good account of himself.

"Okay," said the credit officer, "what have you got for us?"

The CEO confidently answered, "As you requested, here is Zefco's cash flow forecast for the next 12 months. If I may, I'd like to go through it and highlight some of the things that are probably of greatest interest and concern to the bank."

"Be our guest," said the banker.

During the next five minutes, the CEO enumerated the various points that he and the consultant had discussed before driving over to the bank. When he finished, the CEO said, "Is there anything else I can shed light on in the forecast?"

"We're impressed with your presentation, but we need to study the numbers in more detail before we can properly critique the forecast," the loan officer said.

The less diplomatic credit officer, who had reviewed scores, if not hundreds of similar forecasts, remarked, "I'm skeptical that Zefco will achieve the results shown in the forecast. Off hand I'd say you're projecting too rapid a return to profitability. It rarely occurs that way in the real world. Also, I have serious reservations about your ability to forestall the trade creditors. I don't understand how Zefco's vendors could allow the company to accumulate so much debt, and I think Zefco could have a rash of lawsuits on its hands in short order.

"Furthermore, the bank is not interested in financing any more losses at Zefco. We're going to carefully track the company's progress, and if it's not satisfactory we're going to withdraw the bank's support. In fact, we're actively considering putting your accounts receivable on notification (i.e., asking them to remit payments directly to the bank).

As the credit officer continued speaking, the CEO thought to himself, "What the [expletive deleted] does a person need to do to convince this cretin to go along with the program?!"

"With the additional security that you've offered in the form of the tax refund, the bank appears to be collateralized but just barely. We're certainly not going to advance any funds if it means the bank will go into an overloan position again. If Zefco continues to lose money at its present pace for the next few months you might want to consider peacefully handing the keys over to us and walking away. We'll foreclose upon our collateral and liquidate it."

"It'll be a cold day in hell before I do that," the CEO responded angrily. "I'll put Zefco into Chapter 11 before I let you [expletive deleted] have the keys. Look, I spent the past week working with a consultant *you* recommended, doing *exactly* what you asked me to do. I've busted my tail producing this forecast, and *I* do think it's possible to achieve the results shown. And I'm prepared to do battle with you and any other creditors I have to!

"You told me a week ago," the CEO continued, "that the bank would support Zefco if it performed. It sounds like you're trying to renege on that pledge now. I don't think you're being fair, and I'm not going to put up with your inflexible attitude!"

"Let's calm down a little," urged one of the attorneys. "We all want to achieve the same objective here. No one wants to see

Zefco fail. The bank's management wants to see Zefco rehabilitate itself, and it is prepared to continue financing the company along some prudent guidelines."

The CEO fired back, "Well, he [glowering at the credit officer] better give me a little breathing space."

"Could we use one of your private offices for a few moments?" the consultant asked.

"Sure," the loan officer said, and he walked them to another room.

"Can you believe that guy?" the CEO blurted.

"Do me a favor, will you?" the consultant said. "Take a deep breath, sit down and compose yourself. You're letting him get to you. I've seen him do this before; it's a favorite negotiating tactic of his. You've got to understand one of his principal responsibilities is to test how much resolve the management of the bank's troubled borrowers have in wanting to achieve a workable turnaround plan. He's trying to find out if you've got the intestinal fortitude to tough things through."

"You're telling me this is some kind of test?" the CEO said with a look of incredulity.

"Yes, at least in part, I believe it is," answered the consultant. "In addition, he's trying to set you up for future negotiations. He wants you to feel that the bank is doing Zefco a huge favor every time it permits the company to make an important financial decision."

"Well, I don't like his methods," the CEO said. "I don't appreciate his playing mind games with me. I can take all the bad medicine he wants to dispense, but I can't handle deception. I'm too damned literal and gullible for that kind of stuff."

The consultant responded, "All I can say is you've got to continually adapt to different styles and personalities. Are you ready to give it another go?"

"Yes," said the CEO, pausing to take another deep breath. "Let's go back to the meeting."

"I apologize for my outburst," the CEO began. "You can probably tell I've not had much experience in matters such as these, and my emotions temporarily got the better of me. I think I now have a pretty good understanding of the bank's position. Actually, we're not that far out of sync with one another. As I said before, Zefco's bank debt will probably drop once we've initiated the steps we developed last week. I guess all we're really asking the bank to do is remain in place while we work with the other creditors to develop a repayment program. Can we count on your continued support?"

"Provided you can come close to living up to the bottom line numbers you've shown us in the cash flow forecast and there is no dissipation in the value of the bank's collateral, you'll have continued access to the bank's funds," the credit officer replied. "We're obviously not going to make any long term commitments but if Zefco performs, the bank will remain supportive. Like it or not, we're in this situation together. We don't need to become friends, but I do hope we'll develop mutual respect."

"So do I," said the CEO. "We're going to bend over backwards to keep the bank apprised of what's occurring inside and outside of Zefco. If there are any negative developments you'll hear about them directly from me. There really isn't anything else for me to say at this juncture. The next move is yours."

The credit officer said, "I've already indicated that the bank won't permit Zefco to borrow funds in excess of formula. We will accept the tax refund as additional collateral. That means the company will have to clear up the book overdraft position using internally generated funds. Based on the cash flow forecast you've presented, it should be possible to do that within the next few months.

"In substance," the credit officer continued, "Zefco is not asking the bank for financing outside of previously approved limits or collateral margins. If that is also your understanding, we might as well conclude this meeting now. Good luck in your discussions with other creditors."

There being no further business, the participants left the conference room to return to their other duties.

As they drove back to Zefco's offices, the CEO said, "That was another horrible experience. Thank goodness, we didn't show them the worst case scenario. I can now empathize with the poor, unfortunate souls who in another era were sent to debtors' prison for financial indiscretions. I dread to think what the credit honcho would have said if we told him Zefco needed to borrow more money, or it mightn't survive."

The consultant said, "He probably would have flatly turned you down. But let's not dwell on the negatives. You accomplished what you set out to do. The bank agreed, albeit conditionally, to continue financing Zefco. Trust me, having this support will be invaluable when we begin our negotiations with the general creditors in a few weeks."

"Who are they?" the CEO asked.

"General creditors," the consultant answered, "are those which typically extend credit to borrowers on an unsecured basis. They include trade creditors, providers of services, and occasionally banks and other lenders which have not collateralized their loans. The common link among general creditors is that their claims against the assets of the debtor are of the same class."

"What do we want to accomplish at the creditors meeting?" the CEO inquired.

The consultant said, "We're getting a little ahead of ourselves, but let me highlight the purpose of the general meeting of creditors."

The consultant then spent the remainder of the trip back to Zefco presenting the following objectives:

- To provide a brief, oral history of Zefco for those creditors who might not be entirely familiar with the company
- To give a full and complete explanation of the causes of Zefco's financial troubles
- To discuss specific operating and financial problems which have arisen in the past several months and which require immediate attention
- To present the financial condition of the company and the salient facts regarding the company's inability to honor its financial obligations as they become due
- To estimate the value of the business if it were required to be liquidated through a foreclosure by the secured creditors or a bankruptcy proceeding
- To show which secured creditors are in senior positions vis-a-vis the unsecured creditors in the event of a forced liquidation
- To explain the action steps that have been and will be taken by Zefco to achieve a business turnaround

- To relate the bank's willingness to support the company, subject to numerous conditions
- To present the 12-month cash flow forecast
- To give assurance that no unsecured creditors have been or will be given preference over any other
- To ask for a 90-day moratorium on previously incurred unsecured creditor debt while a comprehensive repayment plan is developed
- To request that a creditors' committee be elected to represent the unsecured creditors and to empower the committee to extend the moratorium, if needed, and to negotiate a repayment program on behalf of all unsecured creditors
- To request that independent legal actions against Zefco not be pursued while the temporary moratorium is in effect
- To agree to buy from existing suppliers on a good-funds, COD basis provided that price, quality and service remain competitive, and payment can be made using company checks
- To demonstrate that a turnaround is possible with the patience and forebearance of all parties-in-interest and
- To reiterate that in the event of a forced liquidation, the unsecured creditors would recover little, if any, of what is owed to them.

As they walked from the car to Zefco's offices, the CEO said, "Do you really think we'll be successful in getting that kind of creditor cooperation?"

"Yes, I do," answered the consultant, "but it won't be a piece of cake. It all depends on how hostile Zefco's unsecured creditors are and how convincing we are in presenting the Zefco turnaround story. It isn't likely though that any of the creditors want the company to go belly-up. If they can continue doing profitable business with Zefco on a COD basis, most creditors will probably opt to do so. It is a relatively risk-free way of conducting business."

The CEO said, "Is there any way we can determine and/or defuse the level of hostility among unsecured creditors in advance of the meeting?"

The consultant replied, "Let me answer your question with

another question: How many CEO's of Zefco's major vendors do you know personally and have had a good, longstanding relationship?"

After a few seconds of reflection, the CEO said, "I'd guess there are about four people that would fit that description."

"That's great," the business advisor said. "I'd suggest that before the general meeting of creditors you meet separately with each of those four persons to discuss Zefco's financial troubles and solicit their support. It would be very advantageous if you could persuade them to attend the meeting and volunteer to become members of the creditors' committee."

"That's not a bad idea at all," the CEO said. "I'd better jot that down in my notebook. While we're discussing the informal meeting with creditors, will you tell me a little bit about CMA (the Credit Managers Association) and how it is going to help Zefco?"

"Gladly," the consultant said. "CMA is a widely respected, independent third party that facilitates the resolution of financial conflicts between a debtor and its creditors. The Southern California office has been in operation for over 100 years. CMA does not offer any legal advice, but, because its representatives have been involved in numerous cases, it can suggest how other debtors and creditors have remedied similar problems. Additionally, CMA assists the debtor and creditors in evaluating all of their respective alternatives.

"CMA usually makes the arrangements for the venue of the meetings. If there are 50 or fewer creditors expected to appear at the initial meeting, it can be conducted at the CMA's offices. Otherwise, a conference room at a nearby hotel is usually rented. Since Zefco will pay for the use of the off-site facilities, it would be beneficial to hold the meeting at CMA if at all possible.

"One of CMA's most important roles," the consultant continued, "is to act as moderator of the initial general meeting between the debtor and its creditors, and perform as secretary at subsequent meetings between the debtor and the creditors' committee that has been formed. In this capacity, CMA documents all of the important issues that are discussed at the meetings and then sends bulletins regarding the outcome of the meetings to the parties-in-interest."

"How much does it cost to use their services?" the CEO asked.

"During the course of the negotiations leading up to a plan of reorganization," the consultant answered, "the cash outlay for CMA services is very, very modest—probably under $3,000 for a company of Zefco's size. These out-of-pocket costs are for things like postage, telephone conference calls and copying. Ultimately, CMA receives a certain percentage of the funds that it collects from the debtor and remits to the creditors. A company of Zefco's size would probably pay a fee, pursuant to a plan, of 5 percent of the total funds disbursed to the creditors by CMA. That's not an insignificant amount but, in my opinion, a fair price for the services provided.

"There is one more thing you should know before we meet with CMA. It strongly encourages, but does not require, that a debtor be represented at the creditors' meeting by legal counsel and/or a business consultant—specialists in matters dealing with financial insolvency. CMA makes this recommendation because the creditors usually obtain legal or other advisors to represent them.

"I'm not in complete agreement with CMA on this point. If Zefco is not represented by outside advisors, there is a fair-to-good chance that the company's creditors will also decide to proceed without their own legal counsel and other specialists as well. As I've said before, the opportunity exists to save literally tens, if not hundreds, of thousands of dollars in fees for outside professional services. And, this is the pivot point in the potentially rapid escalation of administrative costs of negotiating an out-of-court reorganization.

"However," the consultant cautioned, *"there are substantial potential risks that Zefco will assume if the company's management is not totally prepared to make a cogent presentation that is accepted by the unsecured creditors.* For example, after hearing your presentation the creditors could decide to attempt to force Zefco into an involuntary Chapter 11 Reorganization or a Chapter 7 Liquidation and seek to replace you with a Trustee.

"Avoiding the use of outside professionals to the maximum extent possible is an abnormally high-stakes business decision, but it may be worthwhile. Most rational unsecured creditors can appreciate having $10,000 to $150,000, or more, remain in the kitty for possible payout to them. We can discuss this further tomorrow when we meet with the CMA officials. Unless we need to discuss some other issues, I think I'll go back to my office. I have a meeting with another client this afternoon."

"That's fine," the CEO said. "I'd better get back to work, anyway."

During the remainder of the day, the CEO involved himself in the usual production, marketing, distribution, financial matters. In addition, he carried out the unpleasant task of firing the individuals identified the previous day.

The next day, the CEO and the business advisor met with CMA officials and related Zefco's financial difficulties in some detail. After about an hour's discussion, CMA's representatives concurred with the consultant's recommendation that Zefco should hold a creditors' meeting as soon as practicable. Reluctantly, CMA also agreed to allow the CEO and his advisor to make their presentation without the presence of attorneys. As is customary, the creditors' meeting was scheduled for 10 days later, to allow sufficient time for the notice of meeting to reach all interested parties. A sample CMA Bulletin is shown in Exhibit 6–1.

The following two weeks passed in a blur as the CEO, his lieutenants and the consultant overturned every stone in an effort to expose and then eliminate waste, inefficiency and other drains on Zefco's profitability. The CMA bulletin was immensely helpful to the CEO and the accounting department. The phone calls from irate credit managers and/or collection agencies wanting payment, stopped almost immediately. Upon receipt of the bulletin, they realized that Zefco was having serious financial problems and the usual collection methods would have little or no effectiveness.

Finally, the day arrived for the general meeting of creditors at CMA's offices. By now, as a result of his total immersion in Zefco's financial difficulties, the CEO had an excellent command of the situation. After brief opening remarks by the manager of CMA's Adjustment Bureau, the CEO was given a chance to

EXHIBIT 6–1

April 3, 1985

In the matter of   )
)
  ZEFCO CONTAINER MFG. CO., INC.   )
  777 El Primero Boulevard   ) BULLETIN NO. 1
  Los Angeles, California 90044,   )
                    Debtor.   )

TO THE CREDITORS:

CREDITORS' MEETING
WEDNESDAY, APRIL 17, 1985 AT 10:00 A.M.
2300 WEST OLYMPIC BOULEVARD,
LOS ANGELES, CALIFORNIA
CONFERENCE ROOM B

(PARKING FACILITIES REAR OF BUILDING. ENTER ON
GRANDVIEW ST.)

This general meeting of creditors has been
scheduled at the request of the principals of the
above business and upon the advice of its financial advisor. The purpose of the meeting is to
review the operating status of the business
and, further, to hear proposals looking toward
the most favorable disposition of creditors'
claims.

Creditors are urged to be in attendance at
this meeting and, in the meantime, are requested
towithhold any independent demands for payment
pending results of said meeting, so that the interests of all concerned may be protected.

Financial information will be made available
at the meeting and immediately thereafter, a

EXHIBIT 6-1 *(Continued)*

```
complete report giving the details and results
of said meeting will be forwarded to all credi-
tors so that even those who cannot attend will
be fully apprised of all of the facts.

                     Yours very truly,



                     Manager
                     Adjustment Bureau
```

---

relate the Zefco story. Working from a detailed outline, he covered all of the crucial points:

- The business history prior to the company's problems
- The specific causes and the nature of Zefco's current financial troubles
- A summary of Zefco's operating results for the past several years as well as a recent condensed balance sheet
- A tentative identification of the various classes of secured and unsecured creditors
- A statement to the effect that if Zefco were to be liquidated in the near future, there would probably be no recovery for the unsecured creditors
- Cash flow projections indicating that a turnaround is possible with patience and forebearance on the part of creditors and
- A promise to pay for future purchases on a COD basis.

Following his presentation, the CEO asked if there were any questions. There are usually few, if any, questions at this point, but there are a number of typical responses:

- Shock and disbelief that the management of the company could allow it to get into such serious financial difficulty
- Anger and frustration that there is no apparent course of action that will result in the immediate payment of creditor claims and

- Resignation to the fact that it will take a concerted effort on everyone's part to help Zefco achieve a turnaround and, thereby, get at least a partial recovery on credit extensions.

The CEO and the consultant were asked to leave the room so that the creditors could discuss the matter in private. About 30 minutes passed before the CEO and his advisor were asked to rejoin the meeting. By this time, the CEO's nerves were pretty frazzled as he imagined himself losing everything. To his great surprise and relief, the CMA official reported that the creditors had agreed to all of Zefco's requests.

By far, the most important of these was the establishment of a creditors' committee with which the CEO could begin negotiating a plan of reorganization on behalf of all unsecured creditors. During the ensuing three-and-a-half months, the Zefco creditors' committee and the company's CEO met several times and had several telephone conference calls to review the progress made in turning the business around, as well as to study in a more in-depth manner the liquidation alternative and the possibility and desirability of selling Zefco to another, financially stronger company. The results of Zefco's negotiations with secured and unsecured creditors are described in the next chapter.

Chapter

7

Preparing and Presenting Zefco's Plan of Reorganization and Disclosure Statement

A successful out-of-court reorganization can, and usually does, mean different things to the parties-in-interest of a financially troubled business. As used in this book, a successful reorganization means that the substance of the business entity continues in existence—ownership of the business may change hands; creditor claims may need to be reduced or even extinguished; assets may have to be sold or redeployed; and executive compensation as well as other facets of the operation may require downward adjustments. However, the bottom line result is that the core business remains intact, profitability is restored, and a significant number of employees are able to continue working and earning a decent living.

A debtor-sponsored plan of reorganization (i.e., one proposed by the owners and managers) can be developed and presented only after the parties-in-interest agree that it is the best alternative to be pursued. It usually requires several months of friendly negotiations between and among the debtor and both secured and unsecured creditors. Liquidation alternatives will have been considered and eliminated—except as a last resort. The sale and/or merger of the business will also have been studied and rejected as a less attractive alternative because the creditors would ultimately receive a lower payback on the debt they hold.

The legal, consulting, accounting and other administrative costs associated with deciding which is the best solution to the problems affecting a troubled business can quite easily run into the *hundreds of thousands of dollars*. The main reason for these high costs is that it can take months of jockeying for position before an effective leader emerges to control the destiny of the business. While this is happening, the meters are running. Much of these costs can be eliminated by a CEO willing and prepared to retain control of the situation.

Naturally, Zefco's management succeeded in its negotiations with all of its creditor groups. After nearly four months of repeated meetings, conference calls and discussions, the company's representatives were ready to present a reorganization plan. The first step was to meet with the critically important secured creditors and assure them that Zefco intended to honor its commitments to them in full. The second step was to meet with the creditors' committee and persuade its members that a viable plan was possible. After a few rounds of negotiations the Zefco Plan of Reorganization was hammered into shape. The plan is presented in its entirety in Exhibit 7–1.

Virtually all out-of-court (informal) reorganization plans take much the same form as the one presented here. It should be read (several times if necessary) until it is fully understood. The comments shown within brackets in the plan are intended to amplify and clarify key elements and generally would not be included in the formal documents comprising a reorganization plan.

EXHIBIT 7-1

ZEFCO CONTAINER MFG. CO., INC.
PLAN OF REORGANIZATION

Zefco Container Mfg. Co., Inc., a California
corporation, (hereinafter called the Debtor),
hereby proposes the following Plan of Reorganization:

I. CLASSIFICATION OF CLAIMS AND INTERESTS.

Class 1: All secured claims against the
Debtor other than secured claims designated in
Class 5 and claims secured by attachment and/or
judgment liens.

[*These are the highest priority claims currently outstanding against
Zefco. They are held primarily by the bank—which has a blanket
security interest in accounts receivable, inventory and certain fixed
assets—and other lenders with chattel mortgages on equipment. Attachment or judgment liens which typically arise as a result of an
unsecured creditor's separate legal action against the company are
treated the same as Class 4 creditors. That is, they are not given a
priority over other creditors that were in similar circumstances. Usually, a
secured lender files a third party claim to preclude payment to unsecured creditors attempting to circumvent a debtor's efforts to reorga-
nize. Occasionally, the only defense against attachments or judgments
is to file for Chapter 11 Bankruptcy.*]

Class 2: All claims against the Debtor which
arose after April 16, 1985, other than those
designated in Class 1 and Class 5.

[*These are unsecured creditors that gave Zefco credit after the moratorium was granted on old debt. Since Zefco has been paying COD for
nearly all purchases there are very few creditors in this class.*]

Class 3: All claims against the Debtor which
arose on or before April 16, 1985 or which are
based upon contracts entered into by the Debtor
prior to that date, other than those designated

ZEFCO PLAN OF REORGANIZATION *(Continued)*

for inclusion in Classes 1, 4 and 5, which are
in the amount of $100 or less or which are re-
duced to $100 at the election of their holders.

[Essentially, any unsecured creditor that has a small claim against Zefco can receive payment in full. The purpose is to eliminate the administrative costs associated with informing and paying these claimants over a protracted period.]

Class 4: All unsecured claims against the
Debtor which arose on or before April 16, 1985
or which are based upon contracts entered into
by the Debtor prior to that date, other than
those designated for inclusion in Classes 1, 3,
5 and 6.

[This is the bulk of Zefco's unsecured creditors and primarily represents trade creditors and vendors of services.]

Class 5: All unsecured claims against the
Debtor held by officers, shareholders and other
"insiders" of the Debtor.

Class 6: The interests of the common shareholders of the Debtor (the Shareholders).

II. SPECIFICATION OF CLAIMS NOT IMPAIRED UNDER
    THIS PLAN.

The claims described in Classes 1, 2 and 3
are not impaired under this Plan. The Plan shall
leave unchanged all of the rights to which the
holders of Class 1 and Class 2 claims are entitled. With respect to Class 3 claims, (i.e.
those of $100 or less including creditors elect-
ing to reduce their claims to $100), the holders
of such claims shall be paid in full upon the Effective Date of this Plan.

[The Plan states that all secured creditors, post-moratorium unsecured creditors and small creditors will be paid everything that is owed to them. The terms and conditions of loan payments may need to be

---

ZEFCO PLAN OF REORGANIZATION *(Continued)*

altered but all principal and interest will eventually be repaid. Generally speaking, any creditor having the power to foreclose on collateral used to secure its loan, and thereby bring a halt to the debtor's business, is able to obtain full payment in out-of-court reorganizations. The debtor and unsecured creditors are usually made fully cognizant of this fact early in the negotiations.]

III. ELECTION TO BE INCLUDED WITHIN CLASS 3.

Any creditor holding a Class 4 claim and desiring instead to be included within Class 3 must, on or before the Effective Date of this Plan, file with the Disbursing Agent (hereinafter defined) a written election to be included within Class 3 and waiving all rights to participate as a Class 4 creditor.

[If, for example, an unsecured creditor that is owed $500 wants to do away with the aggravation of waiting several years to collect its money by reducing the claim to $100, the claim will be settled quickly.]

IV. SPECIFICATION AND TREATMENT OF IMPAIRED CLASSES OF CLAIMS AND INTERESTS.

Class 4: The claims designated in Class 4 shall be paid a minimum of 50 percent of the amounts due. The formula as to the amount and the timing of the periodic payments is described in Section V and Section XI of the Plan.

[This says that the future net cash flow of Zefco's business is probably inadequate to repay all of the unsecured creditors. Additionally, since there is no mention of interest payments, the present value of the future payments is even less than the nominal amounts. Why would the general creditors find this an acceptable payment plan? Because the "liquidation" alternative showed that they would probably recover nothing in that situation.]

Class 5: Class 5 claims shall be paid a <u>maximum</u> of 50 percent of the principal amount due. Class 5 claims shall also be subordinate to

ZEFCO PLAN OF REORGANIZATION *(Continued)*

$800,000 of payments to Class 4 creditors. Upon the Debtor's payments to the Disbursing Agent a total of $800,000 for distribution to Class 4 creditors, plus an amount equal to the fees, costs and expenses to date of the Disbursing Agent, the Class 5 creditors shall thereafter receive payment in accordance with the formula described in Section V of the Plan.

[*The owners of Zefco are saying to the unsecured creditors that Zefco's officers and insiders are also going to suffer. First, they will only get half of the money they loaned Zefco; and, second, they won't be paid back until the other unsecured creditors get half of their funds back.*]

Class 6: The Shareholders shall pledge all of their common stock ownership in the Debtor to secure the Debtor's obligations to Class 4 creditors whose claims are impaired by this Plan. The Debtor agrees not to issue any additional common stock or other equity securities until its obligations under this Plan have been satisfied, except as may be approved by the Creditors' Committee.

[*In other words, if Zefco's managers and owners don't perform, the unsecured creditors will be able to replace them with someone who can. This assumes that Zefco's owners haven't previously pledged their stock to someone else. Additionally, if Zefco hadn't already granted security interests in virtually all of its assets, they, too, would probably be used to secure indebtedness to Class 4 creditors.*]

V.   METHOD, AMOUNT AND TIMING OF PAYMENTS TO CREDITORS IN CLASSES 3, 4 and 5.

Class 3: Payment to Class 3 creditors shall be made on the Effective Date of the Plan. The payment to Class 3 creditors shall be a one-time, lump sum payment.

Classes 4 and 5: The Debtor's payments to creditors in Classes 4 and 5 shall be made from

ZEFCO PLAN OF REORGANIZATION (Continued)

60 percent of the Debtor's net cash flow (as hereinafter defined) until the fifth anniversary date of the first payment to Class 4 creditors, at which time any remaining indebtedness to Class 4 and Class 5 creditors will be extinguished. Class 4 creditors shall receive the first $800,000 paid to the Disbursing Agent for distribution to creditors in Class 4 and Class 5. Thereafter, the Class 4 and Class 5 creditors shall participate on a pro rata basis. Notwithstanding the foregoing, the payments to Class 3 creditors, as provided in this Plan of Reorganization, shall be deducted from the 60 percent of net cash flow otherwise available for the first quarterly installment due Class 4 creditors.

The debtor shall, on or before the fifth business day following the end of each quarter, deposit with the Disbursing Agent, a sum of not less than the minimum payments specified in Section XI hereof. Within 30 days after the end of each quarter, the Debtor shall deposit with the Disbursing Agent such additional sums as may be required to pay 60 percent of net cash flow as hereinafter set forth.

For purposes of this Plan, the Debtor shall have the first quarter end on December 31, 1985. The distribution of any deposits shall be conditioned upon this Plan becoming Effective. Unless and until the Effective Date, the deposits shall be held in trust pursuant to a Trust Agreement implementing this and other provisions of the Plan.

For purposes of this Plan, the term "net cash flow" shall be calculated as follows:

• All cash received by or for the benefit of the

ZEFCO PLAN OF REORGANIZATION *(Continued)*

Debtor excluding: proceeds of loans; and such
other proceeds which the Creditors' Committee
authorizes to be excluded;

- Less cash disbursements for ordinary and
  usual business and prepaid expenses (including the fees, costs and expenses of the Disbursing Agent which are to be paid by the
  Debtor, but excluding the "Performance Compensation" provided in Section X hereof);
- Less cash disbursements to acquire inventory
  and related materials and supplies; provided,
  however, deductions for inventory acquisitions shall be limited to anticipated sales
  for the next ensuing month unless the Creditors' Committee approves a greater deduction;
  and
- Less reasonable reserves for anticipated federal and state income taxes (subject to adjustment when actual tax liabilities are as-
  certained).

[*Since no one really knows how much net cash flow will ultimately be received by Zefco duing the next five years, it was decided that there should be no effort to limit the maximum payments that would be made to Class 4 creditors. To give them
some downside protection, however, a floor of 50 percent of
Class 4 claims was used to induce that creditor class to ratify the
Plan of Reorganization.*]

VI. DISBURSING AGENT.

It is contemplated that the Credit Managers
Association of Southern California ("CMA") will
act as Disbursing Agent hereunder. The Disbursing Agent will receive all payments which are to
be made under this Plan to creditors in Classes
3, 4 and 5 and shall distribute the sums so received, less reserves for disputed claims, as
soon as practical. From and after the Effective

ZEFCO PLAN OF REORGANIZATION *(Continued)*

Date, the Debtor's payments to the Disbursing Agent shall be deemed payments to creditors irrespective of when the Disbusing Agent actually distributes funds to creditors.

The Disbursing Agent's out-of-pocket expenses shall be paid by the Debtor as soon as practicable following presentment of an invoice by the Disbursing Agent. The Disbursing Agent's fees, in addition to its out-of-pocket expenses, shall be computed at the rate of 5 percent of the total payments distributed by it. The aforesaid fees by CMA as Disbursing Agent (as distinguished from its out-of-pocket expenses) shall be deducted by CMA from the quarterly deposits prior to making distributions to creditors.

VII. CREDITORS' COMMITTEE.

A Creditors' Committee was duly elected at a general meeting of creditors of the Debtor on April 17, 1985. Creditors who accept or who are otherwise bound by this Plan nominate, constitute and appoint the individuals who are the present members of said committee and their respective successors, if any, to serve as the members of the Creditors' Committee to administer this Plan for and on behalf of all creditors.

Any member of the Committee may resign by filing a written notice of resignation with either the Chairperson or the Secretary to the Committee. In the event of the death or resignation of any member of the Committee, the business represented by the member who has died or resigned shall appoint a successor member. Unless the successor is appointed within five days after request by the Committee, a majority

ZEFCO PLAN OF REORGANIZATION (*Continued*)

of the remaining members of the Committee may select any person or firm from among the remaining Class 4 creditors to fill the vacancy thus created. The term "Creditors' Committee" or "Commit-tee" as used herein refers to the Committee as constituted at any time, notwithstanding any changes or vacancies.

In the event that a proceeding is commenced by or against the Debtor for relief under the U.S. Bankruptcy Code, and if the Debtor proposes a Plan of Reorganization providing for essentially the same treatment of creditors in Classes 3, 4 and 5 as herein provided, the Committee shall continue, subject to alteration to the membership by appointment of the United States Trustee or by the Court.

CMA shall continue to serve as Secretary to the Committee. In the event that CMA is unwilling or unable to perform the duties as Secretary hereunder, the Committee shall appoint another person or entity to act as such Secretary.

No Committee member shall be entitled to compensation for serving as a member of the Committee. However, the reasonable fees and costs of advisers, accountants and others employed by the Committee as well as the reasonable out-of-pocket expenses incurred by the members of the Committee from and after the Effective Date of this Plan shall be deducted from the quarterly deposits made with CMA prior to making distributions to creditors. The payment obligation of the Debtor, shall include an amount equal to the fees and expenses previously deducted by CMA.

Except as otherwise provided for herein, the Committee shall have the power to adopt its own rules and procedures and may choose one of its members to act as Chairperson.

ZEFCO PLAN OF REORGANIZATION *(Continued)*

The Committee shall act by majority vote of its members. Any member of the Committee shall be entitled to allow another member to vote in his or her stead or behalf at any time. Following written, telephonic or other notice of any meeting of the Committee, any member may at any time before or after such meeting notify the Secretary to the Committee as to his or her position on any particular matter and such notice to the Secretary, whether received in writing, by telegram, orally, by telephone message or otherwise, shall constitute a sufficient basis for counting said member as present at the meeting and for counting his or her vote as so communicated.

The Committee may continue to consult with the Debtor with respect to its performance under this Plan. The Committee's powers shall include, without limitation, the discretion to declare any default under the Plan or under any security agreement or other instrument which may be executed in furtherance of this Plan, to extend the time for curing any default and to refrain from declaring any such default if the Committee determines in its sole discretion that it is not in the best interests of creditors to declare a default.

The Committee may also waive or agree to modify or correct any covenants, conditions and provisions of the Plan and all agreements incidental thereto as the Committee in its sole discretion deems to be in the best interests of creditors.

No member of the Committee shall be liable for any act or omission, including the determination not to declare a default hereunder on his or her part or of any agent, employee or repre-

ZEFCO PLAN OF REORGANIZATION *(Continued)*

sentative of the Committee, or of the Debtor, except for his or her own malfeasance or willful neglect.

No provision of this Plan shall be construed to vest in the Committee (a) title to, trusteeship or control over any assets of the Debtor or (b) any authority or responsibility for the operation of the Debtor's business.

[This section of the Plan of Reorganization is laden with standard boilerplate clauses to set forth the mechanics of how the committee will operate. It needs to be included so that all unsecured creditors know that their interests will be protected and served over the period of time that the Plan is in effect.]

VIII.   <u>SECURITY FOR PERFORMANCE.</u>

As security for the Debtor's performance of its obligations under this Plan, the Shareholders of the Debtor will pledge all of their shares of stock in the Debtor. The Shareholders shall execute such documents and take such other steps as may be necessary to create and perfect the security interest in the stock.

CMA shall perform as the "secured party" under the pledge agreement which is to be furnished under this Plan. CMA shall possess and exercise the rights conferred under the pledge agreement as trustee for all Class 4 creditors.

The security interest being provided by the Shareholders shall be on a non-recourse basis and shall not subject such parties to any liabilities or loss beyond loss of the stock so pledged.

IX.   <u>FINANCIAL REPORTS AND RELATED MATTERS.</u>

The Debtor shall provide CMA and the Creditors' Committee with quarterly statements of

ZEFCO PLAN OF REORGANIZATION *(Continued)*

operation, balance sheets and statements showing a computation of net cash flow. Additionally, the Debtor shall submit, as soon as the
same are available, year-end financial statements "audited" by an independent Certified
Public Accountant (unless such requirement is
waived in writing) as well as all federal and
state income tax returns.

The Debtor shall permit representatives of
the Committee, upon reasonable notice and at
reasonable times, to inspect the books and
records of the Debtor and to monitor its operations. The Debtor shall not be required to allow
access to or inspections of documents, pro-
cesses or other items which are by contractual
agreement to be kept confidential or which constitute trade secrets. The reasonable and necessary costs and expenses incurred by the Committee for such inspection and monitoring shall
be paid by the Debtor in accordance with Section
VII hereof.

X.   <u>EXECUTIVE COMPENSATION AND RELATED</u>
     <u>PROVISIONS.</u>

The Base Salary of Zefco's Chief Executive
Officer will initially be $70,000 per annum.
Annually thereafter, said Base Salary may be
increased by the <u>lower</u> of 7 percent or the year-
over-year change in the Consumer Price Index
for the Los Angeles/Long Beach/Anaheim
metropolitan area. The Base Salaries of Zefco's
other key employees will be scaled down from the
CEO's Base Salary.

In addition to their Base Salaries, and provided that the minimum payments described in
Section XI are being met and that no defaults
exist under the Plan, the CEO and other key em-

ZEFCO PLAN OF REORGANIZATION *(Continued)*

ployees may receive additional "Performance Compensation" not to exceed 8 percent of net cash flow (as defined in Section V hereof), payable not more frequently than the payments made to the Disbursing Agent for the benefit of Class 4 creditors. The CEO shall have full discretion as to the distribution of said Performance Compensation.

The aforementioned limitations upon compensation shall continue until such time as all indebtedness has been repaid to Class 4 and Class 5 creditors or until the expiration of this Plan, whichever first occurs.

Zefco's CEO and other key employees shall also be entitled to reimbursement of business expenses as may be customary and reasonable for businesses having sales levels comparable to the Debtor.

XI. DEFAULT.

The Committee shall have the option of declaring a default under this Plan should the Debtor breach its obligations under this Plan or should the Debtor breach the stock pledge being provided in connection with this Plan.

The Committee shall also have the option of declaring a default under this Plan if the Debtor fails to pay when due the following amounts for two successive quarters or three quarters in any six successive quarters and provided that on a cumulative basis the Debtor is behind on the payments hereinafter set forth:

First Year: $23,000 each quarter; total $ 92,000
Second Year: $30,000 each quarter; total   120,000

ZEFCO PLAN OF REORGANIZATION (Continued)

Third Year:	$39,000 each quarter; total	156,000
Fourth Year:	$48,000 each quarter; total	192,000
Fifth Year:	$60,000 each quarter; total	240,000
		$800,000

The foregoing <u>minimum</u> payment stream shall not be construed as to relieve the Debtor of its obligations to make the payments provided in Section V.

Although an event of default may occur, only the Committee shall have the right to declare a default. Should it do so, it shall notify the Debtor and the Debtor shall have 10 business days within which to cure the default unless the cure period is extended by the Committee. Should the Debtor fail to cure the declared default, the Committee may:

a) report the default, but take no action;

b) waive the default;

c) extend the time to cure the default;

d) instruct CMA to enforce its rights and remedies afforded by the stock pledge agreement; or

e) seek to have entered against the Debtor an order for relief under Chapter 7 or Chapter 11 of the Bankruptcy Code.

XII. <u>EFFECTIVE DATE OF THE PLAN.</u>

In the absence of the commencement of a case under the Bankruptcy Code, the Effective Date of the Plan shall be 30 days after the date that the Debtor receives consents from 80 percent in dollar amount of creditors whose claims are impaired under this Plan or such lesser percentage as the Debtor may deem acceptable.

It is contemplated that by virtue of the sub-

ZEFCO PLAN OF REORGANIZATION *(Continued)*

stantial amount of impaired debt, the Debtor may deem it to be necessary, notwithstanding obtaining consents from creditors holding 80 percent in dollar amount, to seek to bind all creditors through a Plan or Reorganization under Chapter 11 of the Bankruptcy Code which would provide for substantially the same treatment of creditors as is provided hereunder. In such event, the Effective Date shall be 30 days following the date that an order confirming the Chapter 11 Plan of Reorganization becomes final.

If the Chapter 11 Plan is not confirmed, this Plan shall not be deemed Effective for any purpose even though the Debtor may have, prior to the commencement of the Chapter 11 case, obtained consents from creditors holding 80 percent in dollar amount of impaired claims.

XIII. GENERAL PROVISIONS.

The Debtor shall not engage in any transactions with any affiliate unless the transactions are ordinary and/or necessary for the Debtor and are upon terms which are no less favorable than would be the case if the transactions were done with non-affiliates.

A consent to the Plan of Reorganization may be used by the Debtor and deemed to be an acceptance of a Chapter 11 Plan of Reorganization which provides for substantially the same treatment of creditors whose claims are impaired by this Plan.

ZEFCO PLAN OF REORGANIZATION (Continued)

Any notices shall be deemed given when mailed, postage prepaid as follows:

To the Debtor:

Zefco Container Mfg. Co., Inc.
777 El Primero Boulevard
Los Angeles, CA 90044
Attn: Chief Executive Officer

To the Committee:

Credit Managers Association
  of Southern California
2300 West Olympic Boulevard
Los Angeles, CA 90006
Attn: Manager, Adjustment Bureau

AND

Bymor Steel Co.
22300 Wilshire Highway
City of Industry, CA 91746
Attn: President and CEO
[Chairman of the Zefco Creditors' Committee]

Respectfully submitted this 12th day of August 1985.

By: _____
                 Chief Executive Officer
                 Zefco Container Mfg. Co., Inc.

After Zefco's Creditors' Committee has endorsed the Plan of Reorganization, it must be submitted to and voted upon by all unsecured creditors. Although the Plan of Reoganization is probably the most important document that the body of unsecured creditors will want to see, it is not adequate to allow those creditors to make an informed decision on whether or not to vote in favor of the Plan of Reorganization.

Only a very small group of unsecured creditors (the Creditors' Committee) has been involved in negotiations with Zefco. The rest really have no concrete idea of what has transpired during the period from the moratorium (April 17, 1985) until the submission of the proposed plan. CMA has attempted to keep all of Zefco's parties-in-interest informed of major decisions and issues by sending out two previous bulletins, but those missives are also insufficient.

What *is* needed is a packet of data that provides an objective, factual, comprehensive discussion and analysis of Zefco—past, present and future. Such a document is called a *Disclosure Statement* and, after it is prepared CMA again takes an active role in the plan approval process. CMA sends out a bulletin, such as the one shown in Exhibit 7-2, accompanied by the previously discussed Plan of Reorganization, together with the Disclosure Statement shown in its entirety in Exhibit 7-3.

EXHIBIT 7-2

                                          August 22, 1985

In the matter of   )
)
   ZEFCO CONTAINER MFG. CO., INC.)
   777 El Primero Boulevard   ) BULLETIN NO. 4
   Los Angeles,California 90044,)
)
                    Debtor.)
   _____)

TO THE CREDITORS:

URGENT COMMUNICATION. PLEASE RESPOND IMMEDIATELY

   During the past few months, your Creditors'
Committee has participated in a number of meetings with the above captioned company regarding
the repayment of its debts. In attendance at
these conferences were the principals of Zefco,
a financial adviser to the company, and members
of the Creditors' Committee as previously cited
in our earlier communications.

   As a result of the discussions held, we can
report a Plan of Reorganization has been nego-
tiated between your Creditors' Committee and
the debtor's representatives, which Plan carries with it the unanimous endorsement of the
Committee. The Committee urges all creditors to
respond to this communication by returning the
attached Ballot to the Plan to Credit Managers
Association immediately.

   The Committee's endorsement of the Plan was
made after consideration of available information, Zefco's performance during the past sev-

EXHIBIT 7–2 *(Continued)*

eral months and available alternatives including liquidation of business.

The salient parts of the Plan are summarized
below and are more fully detailed in the "Plan
of Reorganization" and the "Disclosure Statement" of Zefco, both of which are enclosed herewith. Creditors are encouraged to carefully review these documents in order to make an
informed judgment.

The Plan of Reorganization takes into consideration approximately $1,700,000 in unse-
cured debt which existed as of April 16, 1985
and, if successful, will entail a minimum payout over time of 50 percent of the amount of the
unsecured debt. Depending upon the future net
cash flow of the company, a 100 percent payout
over time is possible, although not at all certain. For further details regarding payments,
creditors are referred to Section V of the Plan.

For purposes of simplification, the unsecured creditors have been grouped into different classes. In accordance with provisions of
the Plan, Class 3 creditors are defined as those
creditors that are owed $100 or less, or those
creditors who wish to reduce their claims to
$100. Payment to the Class 3 unsecured credi-
tors will be made in full, in cash, upon confir-
mation and funding of the Plan.

Class 4 creditors shall be paid from 60 percent of the debtor's net cash flow for a period
of five years. Any debt remaining at that time
will be forgiven.

Creditors are once again encouraged to review the details of the Plan concerning the minimum payments and to determine which class they
belong to.

EXHIBIT 7-2 *(Continued)*

CMA shall act as Disbursing Agent for the unsecured creditors, with dividend payments to be
made quarterly.

The shareholders of the debtor have pledged
their stock in Zefco as security. CMA, as
trustee for the unsecured creditors, shall be
the "secured party" under the pledge agreement
which is to be furnished as security for the
debtor's performance of the reorganization
plan. It would appear in the best interests of
all creditors to respond to this solicitation
without delay.

Creditors are reminded that this program
carries with it the unanimous recommendation of
the Creditors' Committee, and creditors are
further encouraged to cooperate with this program and continue to withhold any independent
demands for payment. In the event any creditor
requires additional operational and/or financial information, please be assured that CMA
shall make available any materials transmitted
by the debtor to CMA and not heretofore transmitted to all creditors of Zefco.

After completing and returning the accompanying ballot form located at the end of the Disclosure Statement, along with a statement of your
account, please advance your files to the latter
part of September for a report with the assurance
that if any significant developments occur in
the interim, you will be informed accordingly.

Yours very truly,

Manager
Adjustment Bureau

encls.

EXHIBIT 7-3

<u>DISCLOSURE STATEMENT</u>

(Relating to the Plan of Reorganization of
Zefco Container Mfg. Co., Inc.)

TO THE CREDITORS, SHAREHOLDERS AND OTHER
PARTIES-IN-INTEREST OF ZEFCO CONTAINER MFG.
CO., INC., A CALIFORNIA CORPORATION
(HEREINAFTER REFERRED TO AS THE "Debtor"):

IMPORTANT: THIS DOCUMENT CONTAINS INFORMA-
TION WHICH MAY HAVE A BEARING UPON YOUR DECISION
TO ACCEPT OR REJECT THE DEBTOR'S PROPOSED PLAN
OF REORGANIZATION. THEREFORE, IT SHOULD BE
STUDIED WITH GREAT CARE.

CERTAIN OF THE FINANCIAL DATA CONTAINED
HEREIN IS UNAUDITED AND MAY NOT HAVE BEEN PRE-
PARED IN CONFORMITY WITH GENERALLY ACCEPTED AC-
COUNTING PRINCIPLES. HOWEVER, THE MANAGEMENT OF
THE DEBTOR HAS MADE A GREAT EFFORT TO ENSURE
THAT ALL SUCH INFORMATION IS ACCURATE AND
FAIRLY PRESENTED.

NO REPRESENTATION CONCERNING THE DEBTOR OR
ANY ASPECT OF THE PLAN OF REORGANIZATION ARE AU-
THORIZED BY THE DEBTOR OTHER THAN AS SET FORTH
IN THIS DISCLOSURE STATEMENT. ANY REPRESENTA-
TIONS OR INDUCEMENTS MADE TO SECURE YOUR ACCEP-
TANCE WHICH ARE OTHER THAN AS CONTAINED IN THIS
DOCUMENT SHOULD NOT BE RELIED UPON BY YOU IN AR-
RIVING AT YOUR DECISION.

<u>THE COMPANY AND ITS BUSINESS</u>

The Debtor was established in 1956 as Zefco
Can Company. Its original business was that of a
manufacturer of various sizes and types of
metal cans. Between the date of its founding and

ZEFCO DISCLOSURE STATEMENT *(Continued)*

1975, the substance of the Debtor's business changed very little. Although it was marginally affected by the ups and downs in the economy of Southern California, the debtor was consistently profitable.

In early 1975, the Debtor expanded its product lines to include composite containers, which are a combination of a fiber body and metal ends. A strong stimulus for the Debtor's entry into this line of business was the wildly erratic U.S. economy in the mid-1970s. In late 1973, a large number of manufacturers perceived that there were going to be growing shortages of all types of raw materials—including plate steel and tin. Prices shot up dramatically for virtually all commodities as major users stockpiled supplies. All-metal cans became increasingly uncompetitive for smaller producers because they were unable to pass along all of the higher costs—assuming they could obtain the necessary materials. Thus, the Debtor's entry into composites.

The Debtor not only survived the 1974-75 recession, it flourished when "normalcy" returned to the base metals market. Between 1975 and 1980, annual sales increased from $775,000 to $1,884,000; and pre-tax profits rose from $2,000 to $87,000. In 1977, the Debtor changed its name to its present form to reflect the fact that its product line was more broadly based than just metal cans.

In the latter half of 1979, the management of the Debtor was presented with an opportunity to purchase one of its competitors whose owner was preparing to retire. The price, terms and conditions of the acquisition appeared to be very favorable. In 1980 and 1981, the Debtor's com-

ZEFCO DISCLOSURE STATEMENT *(Continued)*

bined entities performed quite well, achieving
record highs in sales and earnings. The Debtor
was apparently on the verge of breaking out of
the entrepreneurial mode of the small business
and joining the ranks of medium-sized businesses.

Also in the early 1980s, the Debtor responded to apparent market forces (and customer
inquiries) that indicated that plastic containers would continue to gain market share in the
container business for the foreseeable future.
A substantial investment was made in expensive,
state-of-the-art injection and blow molding
equipment. With an expanded product line, the
Debtor appeared poised to continue its solid
performance for years to come.

RESULTS OF OPERATIONS

The Debtor now recognizes that it made a major financing error in using borrowed funds almost exclusively to achieve its objective of
becoming a larger competitor in its line of
business. The high interest rates that were
used to reduce inflation in the U.S. in the
early 1980s took their toll on the Debtor's
overextended business.

Exacerbating the recession-induced problems
of the Debtor were the facts that its internal
managerial controls and external accounting
surveillance were deficient. This caused the
Debtor to be tardy in taking corrective action.
As a result of previous CMA bulletins, all
parties-in-interest should be aware of the
Debtor's financial condition and recent operating performance.

ZEFCO DISCLOSURE STATEMENT (Continued)

To refresh your memory, the Debtor's condensed Statements of Operations for the past eight years are shown below (in thousands of dollars):

Year	Sales	Cost of Sales	S, G & A Expenses	Interest and Other Expenses	Taxes (Benefits)	Net Profit (Loss)
1977	1193	931	142	66	25	29
1978	1466	1158	176	62	32	38
1979	1884	1470	217	70	40	87
1980	3807	2975	419	222	88	103
1981	4031	3055	443	328	94	111
1982	4018	3224	482	341	(14)	(15)
1983	4236	3618	508	358	(114)	(134)
1984	4821	4211	627	474	-0-	(491)

During the past four months of operations, the Debtor believes that it has initiated many of the steps needed to achieve a complete business turnaround. Words, however, are of little importance when it comes to repaying debts. The salient facts must be reflected in the "numbers". The Debtor is cautiously optimistic that the trend established in the post-moratorium period will continue for many more months into the future. The Debtor's Statements of Operations for the past seven months are summarized below (in thousands of dollars):

1985	Sales	Cost of Sales	S, G & A Expenses	Interest and Other Expenses	Taxes (Benefits)	Net Profit (Loss)
January	405	356	59	28	-0-	(39)
February	420	370	63	27	-0-	(40)
March	437	385	66	27	-0-	(40)
April	445	385	60	26	-0-	(28)
May	443	381	53	25	-0-	(16)
June	430	365	51	21	-0-	(7)
July	432	363	48	22	-0-	(1)

ZEFCO DISCLOSURE STATEMENT *(Continued)*

NEGOTIATIONS WITH CREDITORS

In late March, 1985, after sustaining significant operating losses, the Debtor's cash
flow situation was critical and its bank, the
primary source of operating funds, had given
indications that it was contemplating the
calling of the revolving loan and term loan
which were then outstanding.

The Debtor then retained a financial consultant to be of assistance in dealing with its
creditors and to preserve the lending relationships with its bank. Shortly thereafter, meetings were held with certain of the major secured
and unsecured creditors and also with officers
of the Debtor's bank for the purpose of attempting to forestall separate creditor actions and
to maintain the bank financing arrangement. The
Debtor was successful in pursuading the bank to
provide ongoing financing on a conditional basis. Moreover, most of the major secured and unsecured creditors indicated that they would cooperate, at least temporarily.

The Debtor then arranged for a general meeting of its unsecured creditors which was held on
April 17, 1985 at the offices of Credit Managers
Association of Southern California ("CMA"). At
that meeting, a Creditors' Committee was
formed.

Numerous meetings were held between the
Debtor and the Creditors' Committee. After considerable effort on the part of many, a Plan of
Reorganization for the repayment of the
Debtor's obligations was agreed to in principle
and subsequently reduced to written form. A
copy of the Debtor's Plan of Reorganization is
enclosed herewith. SAID PLAN OF REORGANIZATION

ZEFCO DISCLOSURE STATEMENT *(Continued)*

BEARS THE UNANIMOUS RECOMMENDATION OF THE CRED-
ITORS' COMMITTEE.

SUMMARY OF PLAN OF REORGANIZATION

The following is a brief summary of the Plan
of Reorganization and should not be relied upon
for voting purposes. Creditors and shareholders
are urged to read the Plan in full. Creditors
and shareholders are further encouraged to consult with legal counsel, if necessary, or with
members of the Creditors' Committee, in order
to fully understand the Plan and its implications.

The Plan does not propose to impair the
claims of secured creditors (other than creditors having attachment and/or judgment liens),
creditors whose claims arose after April 16,
1985, or creditors whose claims as of April 16,
1985 were $100 or less. Secured claims are to be
honored in accordance with the terms agreed
upon. Post-April 16, 1985 claims have been paid
almost entirely on a COD basis. In the future,
new, unsecured claims will be paid in the ordinary course of business or according to terms
otherwise agreed to between the Debtor and the
holders of such claims. Creditors holding
claims of $100 or less (including those who
elect to reduce their claims to $100) will be
paid in cash in full upon the Effective Date of
the Plan.

All other claims against the Debtor which
arose on or before April 16, 1985, are subject
to the repayment and other provisions of the
Plan. These claims are designated as Class 4 and
Class 5 under the Plan. Class 4 claims are esti-

ZEFCO DISCLOSURE STATEMENT *(Continued)*

mated by the Debtor to be in the approximate amount of $1,600,000. Class 5 claims are all unsecured claims held by officers and stockholders of the Debtor in the approximate amount of $100,000.

In essence, Class 4 claims will be paid a minimum of 50 percent of the amount due payable over a five-year period. Depending upon the Debtor's net cash flow (as defined in Section V of the Plan) over the referenced time frame, 100 percent payout is possible, although not probable. In the event that the total amount due to Class 4 and Class 5 claims is not repaid in a period of five years, the Plan provides for any unpaid Class 4 and Class 5 claims to be extinguished (that is, forgiven or reduced to nil).

Creditors in Class 5 will not participate in any distributions, and their claims will be subordinated until such time as payments For Class 4 claims total $800,000. Thereafter, creditors in Classes 4 and 5 will share on a pro rata basis.

Payments for creditors in Class 4 and Class 5 will be made on a quarterly basis to CMA which will serve as Disbursing Agent. The payments shall equal 60 percent of the Debtor's net cash flow. Although not specified in the Plan, the Debtor estimates that its cumulative net cash flow should exceed $3,000,000 during the next five years and, accordingly, Class 4 and Class 5 creditors could be repaid their claims in full. HOWEVER, THESE ESTIMATIONS ARE BASED SOLELY ON THE BEST JUDGMENT OF THE DEBTOR'S MANAGEMENT AND ADVISORS AND COULD BE SUBJECT TO SUBSTANTIAL VARIANCE IN COMPARISON WITH ACTUAL PERFORMANCE. Notwithstanding the foregoing caveat, management firmly believes that the Debtor will

ZEFCO DISCLOSURE STATEMENT *(Continued)*

be able to meet the minimum performance standards under the Plan.

The obligations to creditors in Class 4 are to be secured by all of the Debtor's capital stock (which is to be pledged by the shareholders of the Debtor). With respect to the interests of the common shareholders (Class 6 claims), their rights are being impaired under the Plan in that their stock interests in the Debtor are to be pledged as security for the Debtor's performance under the Plan.

The Creditors' Committee will continue to function throughout the period of the Plan. The Creditors' Committee is given broad powers and discretion under the Plan and therefore specific attention should be given to Section VII of the Plan.

The Plan further provides for limitations upon Executive Compensation to the Debtor's Chief Executive Officer and other key employees (Please refer to Section X of the Plan.)

The Effective Date of the Plan will be thirty (30) days after the date that the Debtor receives approval of the Plan from 80 percent in dollar amount of creditors whose claims are impaired under the Plan or such lesser percentage as the Debtor may deem satisfactory.

It is contemplated that by virtue of the sizable amount of impaired debt, the Debtor may deem it necessary, notwithstanding the obtaining of the necessary consents, to seek to bind all creditors through a Plan of Reorganization under Chapter 11 of the Bankruptcy Code which would provide for substantially the same treatment of creditors as is provided in the Plan. In such event, the Effective Date of the Plan shall

ZEFCO DISCLOSURE STATEMENT *(Continued)*

be thirty (30) days following the date that a confirming the Chapter 11 Plan of Reorganization becomes final.

A CONSENT TO THE PLAN MAY BE USED BY THE DEBTOR AND DEEMED TO BE AN ACCEPTANCE OF A CHAPTER 11 PLAN OF REORGANIZATION WHICH PROVIDES FOR SUBSTANTIALLY THE SAME TREATMENT OF CREDITORS WHOSE CLAIMS ARE IMPAIRED BY THIS PLAN. The purpose of this provision is to protect the Debtor's ability to perform under the Plan. Since there are impaired claims in the approximate amount of $1,700,000, and since the Debtor's net cash flow has only recently returned to a positive position, the Debtor cannot be expected to meet its Plan obligations and, concurrently, satisfy any significant amount of claims of dissenting creditors.

An out-of-court reorganization binds only those creditors who accept the Plan. A Plan of Reorganization confirmed under Chapter 11 proceeding will bind all creditors. It is for the latter reason that the Debtor desires to retain the flexibility of binding all creditors to a Chapter 11 Plan of Reorganization if the Debtor fails to obtain consents from enough creditors that could otherwise undermine the Debtor's ability to perform.

ADDITIONAL SOURCES OF INFORMATION

CMA has acted as Secretary at Creditors' Committee meetings with the Debtor. Minutes of the meetings and conferences and copies of the related creditor bulletins (which were previously mailed to all parties-in-interest) are maintained by CMA. CMA has also been furnished

ZEFCO DISCLOSURE STATEMENT *(Continued)*

with a substantial volume of other data relating to the financial, operational and business
affairs of the Debtor. All of the foregoing information may be inspected by creditors wishing
to view the same prior to making a final decision on whether or not to approve the Debtor's
proposed plan.

CONFIRMATION STANDARD

As previously noted, this out-of-court Plan
will become effective upon receipt by the
Debtor of 80 percent in dollar amount of claims
that are impaired upon the Plan. Nevertheless,
the Debtor may petition to file a Plan of Reorganization under Chapter 11 of the Bankruptcy
Code providing for substantially the same
treatment of creditors. If the Debtor files a
proceeding under Chapter 11 of the Bankruptcy
Code, the Plan must be accepted by creditors
holding at least two-thirds of the amount and
one-half in number of the claims of each class
for which votes are cast.

Additionally, with respect to stockholders,
the Plan must be accepted by holders of at least
two-thirds in amount of the allowed interests
of such class for which votes are cast. However,
in the event that any impaired class fails to
approve the Plan, the Plan may still be confirmed if it does not discriminate unfairly and
is fair and equitable with respect to each non-
approving impaired class.

LIQUIDATION ALTERNATIVE

Below is shown the Debtor's analysis of the
liquidation value of its assets.

ZEFCO DISCLOSURE STATEMENT (Continued)

Liquidation Analysis
As of July 31, 1985

	Net Book Value	Estimated Liquidation Value
Accounts receivable	$ 545,000	$ 410,000
Inventory	556,000	360,000
Plant, property and equipment	2,410,000	725,000
Goodwill and other	425,000	20,000
Total Net Book Value	3,936,000	
Gross Liquidation Value		1,515,000
Estimated Costs of Liquidation at 12%		180,000
Net Liquidation Value		1,335,000
Amounts due secured parties:		
Bank loans	$1,120,000	
Other loans	1,100,000	2,220,000
Secured party deficiency		$ (885,000)
Net amount available for unsecured creditors		-0-
Total creditor claims		$3,906,000
Estimated percentage recovery		-0-

IT MUST BE FULLY UNDERSTOOD THAT THE LIQUI-
DATION ANALYSIS IS BASED SOLELY UPON ESTIMATES
BY MANAGEMENT AND ITS ADVISORS AND IS NOT THE
PRODUCT OF PROFESSIONALS WHOSE METHODS OF ANAL-
YSIS MAY BE MORE COMPREHENSIVE AND WHOSE OPIN-
IONS MAY BE CONSIDERED MORE RELIABLE. HOWEVER,
YOUR CREDITORS' COMMITTEE IS IN BASIC AGREEMENT
WITH THE ANALYSIS AND IT DID NOT DEEM IT NECES-
SARY TO RETAIN INDEPENDENT VALUATION EXPERTS.

MANAGEMENT OF THE REORGANIZED DEBTOR

The Board of Directors, the Chief Executive
Officer and other key employees of the reorganized Debtor are expected to continue to serve
the Debtor in their current capacities. However, the Debtor reserves the right to change
the composition and number of the Board of Di-

ZEFCO DISCLOSURE STATEMENT *(Continued)*

rectors and also to change the officers solely
at its discretion, and without first consulting
the Creditors' Committee. No changes, though,
are anticipated in the immediate future.

CONCLUSIONS

It is the opinion of the Debtor that the inter-
ests of all creditors will be best served if the
Debtor is permitted to perform under the Plan.
The reasons for its conclusion are as follows:

The Plan provides for payment of a substantial amount of the impaired creditor claims;

The tangible assets of the Debtor are likely
to retain most of their value over the life
of the Plan;

Creditors will receive a pledge of the stock
of the Debtor, thus being in a position to
effect future control of the business or,
alternatively, to facilitate a sale of the
business as a going concern;

Class 5 creditors holding claims in the
amount of $100,000 are willing to subordi-
nate same until Class 4 creditors have been
paid $800,000; and

The Debtor very strongly believes it is
highly improbable that unsecured creditors
will receive anything close to what they
would receive under the Plan if the Debtor
were instead liquidated.

Respectfully submitted this 20th day of August,
1985.

By: _____

Chief Executive Officer
Zefco Container Mfg. Co., Inc.

After the unsecured creditors have studied the Plan of Reorganization to their complete satisfaction, they are asked to vote on Zefco's proposal. The ballot, which accompanies the other data sent to creditors, will usually be very similar to the one shown below as Exhibit 7–3. The reader should note that CMA asks each creditor to attach a statement of account to the ballot. The statements of the creditors are then compared to Zefco's own payables records and any disputes that arise are reviewed and resolved.

EXHIBIT 7–4

In the matter of   )
)
  ZEFCO CONTAINER MFG. CO., INC.,)
  777 El Primero Boulevard   )
  Los Angeles, California 90044,   )
)
                              Debtor.   )
———————————————————————————)

BALLOT FOR ACCEPTING OR REJECTING
PLAN OF REORGANIZATION

    (1) The undersigned is a creditor of Zefco Container Mfg. Co., Inc.

    (2) Having received and reviewed the "Plan of Reorganization", dated as of August 12, 1985 and its accompanying "Disclosure Statement", dated August 20, 1985 the undersigned hereby (check box):

    a. (   ) Accepts or b. (   ) Rejects the Plan.

(   ) <u>Class 3</u>: Creditors with claims as of
                  April 16, 1985, $100 or less, and
                  creditors who wish to reduce
                  their claim to $100 shall be paid
                 · in full, in cash, upon confirma-
                  tion and funding of the Plan.

EXHIBIT 7-4 *(Continued)*

(   ) <u>Class 4</u>:   Creditors with claims as of April 16, 1985, over $100 shall be paid a <u>minimum</u> of 50 percent of the amounts due, from future net cash flow, through quarterly distributions over five years, in accordance with the Plan.

In the event a petition is filed under Chapter 11 of the Bankruptcy Code, the undersigned's vote accepting or rejecting the Plan and the selection of the repayment option on this ballot shall be deemed to have been the undersigned's vote and selection under any Plan filed in such case, which proposes payment to creditors upon terms which are not materially different from those set forth in the Plan.

DATED: _____

AMOUNT OF CLAIM: $_____
(as of April 16, 1985)

    CREDITOR: _____

    BY: _____
(Authorized Representative)

    ADDRESS _____

    CITY _____ STATE _____ ZIP ____

Please complete this form, attach statement of your account thereto, and return immediately to:

ADJUSTMENT BUREAU
Credit Managers Association of
Southern California
P.O. Box 20915
Los Angeles, California 90006

Once the necessary votes are obtained (80 percent in Zefco's case), the arrangement is complete. Zefco can go about the business of completing the turnaround. Considering the results that are possible, and the unpleasant alternatives, it is clearly well worth the effort to try and get an out-of-court reorganization.

The real world resolution of tough financial problems doesn't always turn out as well as it did for Zefco. In the final chapter we will discuss the court-supervised turnaround process.

Chapter

8

Using the Protection of the Bankruptcy Court if All Else Fails

As might be concluded from the methods recommended for dealing with financial adversity discussed throughout this book, filing for protection under Chapter 11 of the Bankruptcy Code is the *last* resort that should be sought by a debtor in a serious financial predicament.

The most compelling reason for addressing business problems in the pro-active manner described in this volume is that most of the steps will be required of the owners and managers either in *or* out of Chapter 11. There is simply no way to avoid the hard work and anxieties associated with a business turnaround.

The steps needed to develop a plan of reorganization and a disclosure statement, under the protection of the court, are very similar to the out-of-court process described in this book. Although there are certain to be some people who might argue differently, I believe the principal difference is the formal structure of the court-approved procedure and the need for attorneys to plead the company's case.

If you allow attorneys, consultants, accountants and others to do the work for you, it will likely cost $50,000 to $250,000, assuming your business has an annual volume of about

$5,000,000. It will be proportionately higher or lower depending on the seriousness of the financial condition of the debtor, sales volume, the number of creditors, the relative strength of the secured and unsecured creditors and other factors.

In addition to the sizable (usually front-end) outlays for professional services, there are a number of other clerical and administrative headaches that must be dealt with if you enter a Chapter 11 proceeding. They include, but are not limited to:

- Filing a list of the 10 largest unsecured creditors at the time of the bankruptcy petition.
- Filing, *within two working days,* a projected operating statement for the first thirty days of operation under Chapter 11.
- Closing all existing bank accounts and opening new accounts *immediately* upon the filing of the petition. The new bank accounts, which must bear the inscription "Chapter 11 Debtor-in-Possession," must include general, payroll and tax accounts.
- Closing the company's books and records *as of the filing date* and opening new books and records for subsequent operation of the business.
- Procuring and filing, *within two days,* a physical inventory.
- Preparing and filing separate statements *for each bank account for each day in which checks are drawn.*
- Filing *weekly* operating reports unless in the circumstances less frequent reporting is deemed warranted; however, the operating reports *must* be filed at least once a month.
- Obtaining prior written authorization of the United States Trustee for the employment and compensation by the company of all officers, directors, shareholders or professionals. [In other words, the business owners/managers face the possibility that they may be unable to remunerate themselves at the same level after filing the bankruptcy petition as before. And they may not have the ability to hire others at will. For privately owned businesses, which employ several family members, this can cause substantial financial hardship not to mention increased emotional and physical trauma.]
- Procuring the consent of the secured creditor(s) or court au-

thorization to use "cash collateral." (This effectively means the owners/managers may well have to survive on even *less net operating cash flow* than was being generated prior to entering Chapter 11.)

The failure to file the schedules and reports required in a bankruptcy case could result in the judge's dismissing the case—the assets of the business would then probably be foreclosed upon or liquidated. In essence, a company operating in a Chapter 11 Bankruptcy proceeding is figuratively placed under a financial microscope. Every meaningful management decision is magnified and subjected to possible criticism by the court and creditors. An us-versus-them mentality predominates during meetings and the margin for error is slim.

Quite frankly, it is all too frequently an extremely uncomfortable and stressful situation for everyone involved and, as oft-repeated in this book, should be avoided if at all possible.

Although the arguments in favor of developing and implementing an out-of-court reorganization plan and business turnaround program are persuasive, there *are* several occasions when a Chapter 11 petition must be filed if the business is to survive and be successfully reorganized. Among others, such "triggers" include:

- Secured and/or unsecured creditors who are so skeptical that incumbent management is competent to achieve a business turnaround that they insist that the business be sold or liquidated rather than reorganized as proposed by the debtor.

- Lawsuits may be filed by secured and/or unsecured creditors who are not in favor of accepting an "unsupervised" (out of court) moratorium on debt repayment or a plan of reorganization. For example, a very well secured creditor might actually want to see the debtor operating under the watchful eye of the court to ensure that its security interests are not dissipated by further management errors.

- Various unsecured creditors holding substantial claims may independently seek writs of attachment, judgment liens or other legal forms of collecting debts owed them. Unless the debtor's principal secured creditor (usually its bank or finance company) files third party claims, the litigious creditors could have the court order successfully executed. Once one link in the fragile chain is broken, the debtor will have enormous difficulty resisting a bankruptcy filing.

- In out-of-court reorganization plans a majority of unsecured creditors cannot bind even a single dissident creditor to accept a debtor proposal. In a Chapter 11 proceeding, however, individual creditors or small groups of creditors who disagree with the majority can be compelled to accept the Chapter 11 plan if it provides them with a higher payout than would be received if the business were liquidated. Typically, a simple majority in number and two thirds in dollar amount of all creditors can approve a Chapter 11 plan. This provision of the Bankruptcy Code is quite powerful in dealing with relatively small unsecured creditors who might attempt to hold large unsecured creditors "hostage" by threatening to prevent the debtor from consummating an out-of-court plan of reorganization.

- It is virtually impossible for a small or medium-sized business with a sizable amount of debt to continue to operate without the protection of the court, if its primary secured lenders decide to stop advancing funds or opt to foreclose on collateral crucial to the operation of the business (i.e., accounts receivable, inventory and/or equipment). Under Chapter 11, an automatic injunction is created by the court prohibiting creditors from enforcing their claims against the debtor. While this stay, or moratorium, is in force secured creditors cannot foreclose on their collateral. This gives the debtor time to develop a plan.

- Chapter 11 allows the debtor to obtain super priority financing, which provides a creditor advancing new funds on a postpetition basis, with a security position that is senior to all previously incurred debt.

- The ability to reject certain executory contracts (for example, burdensome leases and collective bargaining agreements) is also a powerful facet of the Bankruptcy Code.

It is, indeed, a great comfort to know that a business in grave financial difficulty can obtain temporary relief from dunning creditors by filing under Chapter 11. But, let the petitioner beware. Debtor-in-possession bankruptcy is not a panacea.

Chapter 11 cannot solve even the most basic financial, marketing or operational problems of a business experiencing a continual flow of red ink. It is, however, an enormously powerful legal tool that affords a debtor a viable alternative to handing over the keys to the bank or finance company, or a liquidation of the business which causes great losses to employees, creditors and shareholders alike.

If it becomes necessary to seek court-provided relief under Chapter 11, do so vigorously. By definition, filing Chapter 11 means that a debtor has not been able to reach an out-of-court settlement or rearrangement with one or more classes of creditors. It also means that one or more potentially hostile adversaries is bent upon preserving or protecting its own turf—usually to the detriment of the debtor or some other creditor class. There are several steps to consider before filing a bankruptcy petition:

- Discreetly inquire about the best, most experienced insolvency lawyers in your area. Don't try to save a few hundred (or even a few thousand) dollars by retaining (that means payment of big fees in advance) attorneys who are not specialized in bankruptcy litigation.

- Provide these new counselors with all documentation relating to security agreements, loan agreements, stock purchase agreements, etc. It happens in almost every case—shoddy documentation on the part of creditors or their attorneys leads to vulnerabilities and willingness to negotiate.

- With as much lead time as possible before filing, start building a war chest of cash. One quickly finds that one can't have too much of this commodity. If the business' primary source of funds is also the creditor forcing the Chapter 11 petition, open a small account at another bank.

- Cancel all purchase orders and start developing a things-to-do list. In other words, circle the wagons and get ready for the attack.

- Be prepared to make rapid decisions regarding the closure or suspension of business activities which are not being operated with positive net cash flows.

- Prepare a current, detailed balance sheet, agings of accounts-payable and a schedule of inventory and fixed assets.

- Help prepare your attorney so that he or she can argue strenuously for the use of cash collateral if your principal source of funds decides that it no longer will support the company and intends to foreclose on its collateral, primarily accounts receivable. It requires a great amount of savvy and finesse to deal successfully with this sensitive subject. *And it requires a well trained, highly experienced legal advisor.* Don't lose your company because you sent an inexperienced attorney to do battle with the lender's legal counsel.
- Look for legal ways to protect personal assets. It will be difficult because owner/managers of small and medium-sized businesses have probably already used personally owned assets to shore up (collateralize loans for) the failing business.
- Lastly, if none, or not all, of your personally owned assets have been used previously to secure loans, do not offer them in a time of crisis.

A comprehensive treatment of a Chapter 11 bankruptcy case is far beyond the scope of this book, and I defer to the professionals to dispense legal advise. Nevertheless, you should be made aware of a few additional legal factors.

For example, who will run the company if Chapter 11 is filed? Will a "trustee" be appointed or will the debtor remain in charge? In the vast majority of bankruptcy cases, the courts will need to find good cause, including fraud, dishonesty, incompetence, or gross mismanagement by a debtor, before a trustee can be appointed in place of the existing management.

Such causes are usually very difficult to prove without lengthy investigation. And, again, expert legal guidance and representation can protect debtors from vindictive creditors bent on seeing that the business fails.

What is an *involuntary* bankruptcy petition? When dissenting creditors do not accept a debtor's out-of-court proposal for reorganizing a business, they can team up to force the debtor into a bankruptcy proceeding—and it's not very difficult. Three creditors with unsecured claims in the amount of $5,000 or more, can initiate an involutary bankruptcy case. This does not necessarily mean that the debtor is being forced into a liquidation. It simply allows the debtor and creditor to have the ability to arrive at a court-directed arrangement.

If the bankruptcy court dismisses an involuntary petition, the court may make the filing creditors pay court costs and any damages. In instances of a bad faith filing, the court might grant compensatory or punitive damages. The potential liability for dismissed petitions may deter creditors from taking legal action without first determining the facts.

How much does it cost to file a Chapter 11 petition? Each petition filed with the bankruptcy court must be accompanied by a *$200* filing fee. Mere peanuts in the whole context of a bankruptcy proceeding. And, believe it or not, a petitioner can apply for permission to pay the filing fee in installments.

During the first 120 days of a Chapter 11 proceeding, the debtor has the *exclusive* right to file a plan of reorganization with the bankruptcy court. If the debtor does not file a plan in the specified period or, having done so, is unable within 180 days to obtain acceptance of the plan from each class of impaired claims, then any party-in-interest (the debtor, creditors, stockholders) may present a plan for consideration by the court. In certain cases the debtor can obtain a 180-day extension.

In the final analysis, the constituent parts of a successful plan of reorganization, whether achieved out of court as advocated in this book, or under the aegis of the Bankruptcy Code, requires that a financially ailing business follow pretty much the same path:

- A creditors'committee must be formed.
- Creditors must be classified and prioritized as to the types of claims.
- Creditors whose claims are *not* impaired by the plan must be specified.
- Creditors whose claims *are* impaired by the plan must be specified.
- A repayment program must be put forth.
- A method of payment must be determined.
- The plan must be approved by *all* creditors whose claims are impaired by the plan.

If the worst case were to happen (the business were to fail and be liquidated), would the owners/managers of a small or medium-sized, privately owned business lose everything? Almost. The U.S. Bankruptcy Code exempts from creditor claims: $7,500 of equity in a debtor's residence (unless the asset was previously used to secure the repayment of a loan); $1,200 of equity in a debtor's motor vehicle; up to $4,000 of accrued interest in an unmatured life insurance policy; and the debtor's interest in certain household furnishings, clothing and appliances. Some states have higher dollar amount exemptions and debtors can choose such exemptions. In short, you can expect to end up damned poor but not penniless, and walk away with the shirt on your back.

The crucial question is "Should the CEO and management lead the turnaround effort or should they allow their outside advisors to lead the way?" I clearly favor the former option and hope that after reading this book you will concur with my opinion.

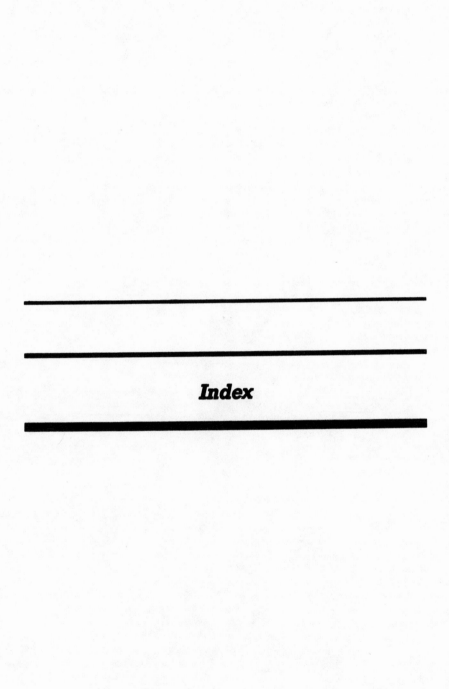

Index

Notes

Notes

Notes

Notes

Notes

Notes

DATE DUE

NOV 1 8 1993			